Translation Practices E

MW00852465

Translation Practices Explained is a series of coursebooks designed to help self-learners and teachers of translation.

Each volume focuses on a specific type of translation, in most cases corresponding to actual courses available in translator-training institutions. Special volumes are devoted to professional areas where labour-market demands are growing: court interpreting, community interpreting, European-Union texts, multimedia translation, text revision, electronic tools, and software and website localization.

The authors are practising translators or translator trainers in the fields concerned. Although specialists, they explain their professional insights in a manner accessible to the wider learning public.

Designed to complement the *Translation Theories Explained* series, these books start from the recognition that professional translation practices require something more than elaborate abstraction or fixed methodologies. The coursebooks are located close to work on authentic texts, simulating but not replacing the teacher's hands-on role in class. Self-learners and teachers are encouraged to proceed inductively, solving problems as they arise from examples and case studies. The series thus offers a body of practical information that can orient and complement the learning process.

Each volume includes activities and exercises designed to help self-learners consolidate their knowledge and to encourage teachers to think creatively about their classes. Updated reading lists and website addresses will also help individual learners gain further insight into the realities of professional practice.

Anthony Pym
Series Editor

Introduction to Court Interpreting

Holly Mikkelson

Routledge
Taylor & Francis Group

LONDON AND NEW YORK

First published 2000 by St. Jerome Publishing

Published 2014 by Routledge
2 Park Square, Milton Park, Abingdon, Oxon OX14 4RN
711 Third Avenue, New York, NY 10017, USA

Routledge is an imprint of the Taylor & Francis Group, an informa business

© Holly Mikkelson 2000

ISBN 13: 978-1-900650-30-4 (pbk)
ISSN 1470-966X (*Translation Practices Explained*)

Cover design by
Steve Fieldhouse, Oldham, UK

Typeset by
Delta Typesetters, Cairo, Egypt

British Library Cataloguing in Publication Data
A catalogue record of this book is available from the British Library

Library of Congress Catalging-in-Publication Data
Mikkelson, Holly.
 Introduction to court interpreting / Holly Mikkelson.
    p. cm. -- (Translation practices explained, ISSN 1470-966X)
Includes bibliographical references.
 ISBN 1-900650-30-4 (pbk. : alk. paper)
 1. Court interpreting and translating. I. Title. II. Series.
 K2155 .M55 2000
 347'.016--dc21
                          00-010131

Dedicated to my father, Vernon Edward Mikkelson, MD
December 9, 1922 – March 23, 2000

Acknowledgements

I would like to acknowledge the colleagues around the world who have so generously contributed to my understanding of their countries' judicial systems and court interpreting practices. I will not name them, for there are so many that I fear I may inadvertently overlook someone. I am particularly grateful to my colleagues in Argentina, Austria, Australia, Germany, Japan, South Africa, Spain and the United Kingdom, who kindly answered my many questions and in some cases even took me to observe court proceedings. Special thanks go to Thomas L. West III, JD, who critiqued the chapters on the law and legal systems.

Finally, I would like to thank my husband, Jim Willis, for his editing assistance, humour and patience.

Holly Mikkelson
June 2000

Contents

1. Introduction

> Between the educated lawyers and the fumbling defendants, perched
> precariously on a bar stool, is the court interpreter.
>
> Rosemary Moeketsi (1999b:13)

Scope and Objective

The purpose of this book is to introduce you to the profession of court interpreting. Like many interpreting specialties, this field is very complex and requires familiarity with a number of subjects, including law, translation and interpretation theory, linguistics, intercultural communication, anthropology, and psychology. It would be impossible to cover all such subjects in depth; the intent of this book is to present an overview of the field and alert teachers and students to avenues for further inquiry.

Court interpreters work not only in courts of law but also in law offices, law enforcement agencies, jails and prisons, and other public agencies associated with the judiciary. They may be known by a variety of names, including legal interpreters, judiciary interpreters, and forensic interpreters. In this book court interpreter/interpreting will be the primary term, although others are used as the occasion requires. All of the settings mentioned above will be addressed throughout the book.

Role of the Court Interpreter

It is generally acknowledged that the role of the interpreter in the judicial setting is to make communication possible despite language barriers that exist between litigants and court personnel. It is a widely recognized principle of law that anyone accused of a crime is entitled to be informed of the charges and allowed to put on a defence. If that person does not speak the language of the court system in which he is being tried, in most countries he has a right to an interpreter. The right to an interpreter in non-criminal cases is not as widely recognized. In any event, the interpreter is viewed as an equalizer, someone who will put litigants who do not speak the language of the proceedings on an equal footing with those who do.

Despite the almost universal right to an interpreter in criminal cases, most countries do not have laws specifying who is qualified to act as an interpreter in court proceedings. In places where multilingualism is very common among the educated classes, traditionally an attempt would be made to find a lawyer who spoke a foreign litigant's language. Thus, a German tourist involved in an auto accident in Denmark would be assigned a German-speaking lawyer for court appearances, and the lawyer would be expected to keep the client apprised of what is said in Danish in the courtroom. Today a greater diversity of languages is spoken by foreign visitors and immigrants, and more explicit provisions are made for the rights of linguistic minorities. Thus, an Albanian-speaking refugee accused of murder in Denmark is not likely to find a Danish lawyer who speaks his language, and, in any case, would need more than an occasional summary interpretation to follow the proceedings and participate actively in his own defence. As more and more languages come in contact in our ever-shrinking world, and as prosecution and litigation become increasingly complex, the importance of competent interpreting services is also becoming more obvious.

What constitutes competent interpreting in the legal sphere is not a simple question. Recent writings on interpretation theory indicate that any sort of interpreting is far more involved than merely transferring words from source language (the language of the original message) to target language (the language into which the message is interpreted). The linguistic aspect of the task alone is a complicated process of decoding, abstracting, and encoding; and the cultural and social aspects of communication must also be considered. For the court interpreter, the task is rendered even more difficult by the gap between different legal systems and the hidden agendas often associated with lawsuits. For example, when a judge asks a Hmong refugee whether he is willing to give up his right to a speedy jury trial, the challenge for the interpreter is to convey the concepts of "rights" and "jury trial" to a person from a remote mountain region untouched by the trappings of a modern justice system, and to do so efficiently in order to elicit a meaningful response from the defendant and enable the judge to get through her busy calendar.

Judicial systems throughout the world are often criticized for being inaccessible to the citizens they are designed to serve. Even in countries where public proceedings are the norm, laypersons who observe or participate in court cases are frequently confused and mystified by the language and behaviour of legal professionals. In many societies, lawyers are reviled for their tendency to obfuscate and manipulate by using arcane language. It is often noted that the court interpreter's role is to level the playing field by overcoming the language barrier, not to put the interpretee at an advantage over other litigants. In other words, the interpreter is not there to make sure the client understands, but merely to give him the same chance anyone else in his place would have if he spoke the language of the court. Thus, a judge's admonition should sound just as intelligible – or unintelligible – to the foreigner listening to the interpretation as it does to a layperson who speaks the official language of the court. What this means is that court interpreters must master not only the techniques of interpreting and a wide range of registers in all their working languages, but also the complexities of the different legal systems and the "legalese" employed by judges and attorneys in those languages. Interpreters must also become adept at maintaining neutrality as they navigate between the Scylla and Charybdis of defence and prosecution, especially in adversarial judicial systems.

Standards for what must be interpreted vary from one country to the next. In the United States, for example, interpreters are expected to interpret simultaneously every word that is uttered in the courtroom, no matter who the speaker is, when a non-English-speaking defendant's case is being heard (this would include jokes and asides, comments about other cases, and the like). In Japan, in contrast, the interpreter is usually not allowed to provide a simultaneous interpretation of the proceedings, but interprets summaries of evidence consecutively. In some courts, the interpreter merely provides a consecutive interpretation of the judge's summary of the proceedings after they have concluded. Often there are no guidelines for interpreters, who are left to determine for themselves what the defendant or witness should hear. In countries where defence counsel are allowed to act as interpreters, it is obvious that the defendant will receive only a summary interpretation at best.

There are also different opinions regarding how far the interpreter should go in bridging cultural and social gaps in the court environment. At one end of the spectrum are those who advocate strict adherence to the linguistic elements of the message and omission of nonverbal elements such as hand gestures, facial expressions, and tone of voice. In this school of thought, interpreters are barred from explaining, elaborating, or clarifying. Particularly in the adversarial atmosphere of common-law jurisdictions, it is argued that efforts by an interpreter to represent or explain cultural aspects of a message would "tamper with a witness's credibility" and affect the opinion the triers of fact may have of the speaker (González et al 1991:483).

At the other end of the spectrum are those who contend that the cultural gaps are sometimes so broad that focusing exclusively on the linguistic aspects fails to convey meaningful information and serves no purpose. In the case of the Hmong refugee cited above, proponents of the first approach would have the interpreter find the closest possible linguistic equivalents to "right" (perhaps a phrase like "privileges to which you are entitled") and "jury trial" ("members of the community deciding if you committed the crime") and leave it up to defence counsel to provide further explanation, or to the defendant to request an explanation. The second school of thought would favour intervention by the interpreter to give a brief explanation of the legal system in language the defendant could understand prior to interpreting the judge's statement. When there is a tremendous disparity in the level of sophistication of legal professionals and laypersons, many of whom are illiterate and have no legal counsel, the "universal ethical and professional principles [of neutrality and impartiality] are a mere ideal situation that may be impossible to achieve" (Moeketsi 1999a & b). Most interpreters take a position somewhere between these two extremes, and every case must be judged according to the circumstances. These issues are examined in more detail in Chapters 4 and 5; suffice it to say that court interpreters must be aware of the impact of culture on language, and must exercise good judgement in reflecting that impact in their interpreting.

History of Court Interpreting

No one knows when interpreting began, but it surely dates back further than recorded history. It is safe to assume that the practice of court interpreting is almost as old as the practice of law. In relatively modern history, Sherr (1999) traces court interpreting in the Spanish-speaking world back to the colonization of the Americas, when as early as the 1500s there were laws stipulating the use of interpreters. Similarly, Moeketsi (1999b) notes that court interpreting in South Africa "dates back to the 17th century when the colonialists first set foot on our shores". Colin and Morris (1996) cite interpreted trials in 1682 and 1820 that were landmarks in English jurisprudence. The first, *Borosky and others*, was a murder trial involving several languages. Colin and Morris note that "when it came to deciding about who was entitled to an interpreter, class – not linguistic need – was the decisive factor. The person who speaks the best English is the aristocrat – and he gets the best treatment from the court" (1996:177). The second case cited by Colin and Morris, the 1820 adultery trial of Queen Caroline, provided examples of interpreters not only rendering the linguistic content of witness statements, but also explaining cultural differences.

Perhaps the most famous interpreted trials in history were those of the Nazi war criminals at Nuremburg in 1945-46. This event is regarded as a watershed for the interpreting profession because it was the first instance of the use of equipment to provide simultaneous interpretation. The Charter of the International Military Tribunal provided, in Articles 16 and 25, that to assure the defendants of a fair trial, the proceedings had to be translated into a language they understood. In addition, the members of the International Military Tribunal represented all the countries of the victorious Allies, and did not share a common language. And finally, as Gaiba (1998:33) points out, "The Nuremberg Trial was one of the first major international media events, and there was the need to keep the international public constantly informed". For all these reasons, it was decided that the only way to conduct these multilingual proceedings efficiently was by using simultaneous interpretation.

Recruiting qualified interpreters in the four working languages of the trial was a monumental task. An initial screening was conducted to identify individuals with fluency in two languages in a wide variety of subjects; those who passed the screening were asked to interpret in a mock trial. Because no one had ever been trained in simultaneous interpreting, few candidates passed this portion of the test. As Gaiba (1998:47) notes,

> Given the stressful conditions of the job, interpreters had to have self-composure under pressure and the ability to concentrate in difficult situations. The job required the mental agility to hear and speak at the same time, and to adapt instantaneously to the stimulus of the source language. This means that interpreters had to be able to quickly find an alternative if the best translation did not come to mind, as they were not supposed to stutter or stop. They had to be able to make decisions quickly and accurately. The job also required great mental and physical efforts because of the need to interpret both speedily and accurately, and to adapt to the speed of the speaker. Finally, interpreters were required to have a good voice and clear enunciation, so that it would be easy to listen to them for hours at a time.

Only five percent of the people tested, including experienced consecutive interpreters, were able to perform adequately (Gaiba, 1998:48). The individuals selected in this screening process were then given several weeks of training, which consisted of interpreting mock trials and receiving feedback on their performance. The training programme continued throughout the trial as new candidates were identified. There was a high turnover among interpreters in Nuremberg because of the horrifying nature of the evidence. Nevertheless, many went on to pursue careers as international conference interpreters.

These accounts of historic trials show that although many talented and competent individuals have provided interpreting services in courts of law over the centuries, court interpreting was never recognized as a full-time occupation. Only recently has the profession been practised by individuals who have chosen court interpreting as a career and received specialized training in it. Even today, many veteran court interpreters began working in the field by accident, because they happened to speak a certain language that was required for a court case, and they learned the techniques of interpreting "by the seat of their pants". As standards rise and consumers of interpreting services become more sophisticated, newcomers to the profession find that formal training is necessary to enter the field.

The first regulation of the quality of interpretation in the judiciary began in the late 1970s. Sweden was among the first European nations to regulate the practice of interpreting, introducing a state authorization exam in 1976 (Ozolins 1998). In the United States, the Federal Court Interpreters Act of 1978 required that Spanish interpreters working in the federal courts demonstrate proficiency by passing a certification exam (González et al 1991). At the same time, the Registry of Interpreters for the Deaf (RID) developed a legal skills certificate as a complement to the general certification exam it had been administering since

1972. Australia began requiring a proficiency exam for interpreters in 1978, Canada in the early 1980s. Several individual states in the U.S. followed the lead of the federal courts and adopted certification requirements for court interpreters. California, for example, began testing interpreters in 1979, followed by New York (1980), New Mexico (1985), and New Jersey (1987). This trend accelerated in 1995 when the National Center for State Courts founded a consortium of states to pool resources for interpreter training and testing.

In many countries, although there has been increasing awareness of the need to ensure the quality of interpreting services in the judiciary, legislatures have not taken action to impose standards; instead, the selection of interpreters has been left to the courts' discretion. In the United Kingdom, for example, the police and the courts are encouraged to employ interpreters listed on the National Register of Public Service Interpreters or other similar lists, but the law does not require them to do so (Colin and Morris 1996; Tybulewicz 1997). As Corsellis (1995:6) points out, "Requirements relating to the provision of interpreters are part of the common law (i.e., law as laid down by the judges) and are not set out in an Act of Parliament". In countries where there is traditionally an occupation of public translator or sworn translator, legislatures have simply declared that these translators are by definition qualified to interpret in court proceedings, even if they have never had any training in interpreting (Valero-Garces 1998; Martonova 1997). It is noteworthy that, whereas in some countries the regulation of court interpreting was initiated by the legislative or judicial branch of government (often with input from professional interpreters), in others, the impetus has come from professional associations themselves.

An additional sign of the growing professionalization of judiciary interpreting is the emergence of professional associations. In the United States, the first such organization to be established was the California Court Interpreters Association (CCIA), founded by a group of interpreters in Los Angeles in 1971. The CCIA played a key role in pushing through the legislation that led to the first certification exam in California in 1979. Independently, the Court Interpreters and Translators Association (CITA) was founded in New York in 1978. In 1988 the organization changed its name to the National Association of Judiciary Interpreters and Translators. Meanwhile, the American Translators Association (ATA), founded in the 1950s, began attracting more interpreter members, and many of its regional chapters and affiliated organizations had large contingents of court interpreters among their membership. In 1998, the ATA started an Interpreter's Division to meet the needs of members who provide both interpreting and translating services. Many states now have professional associations that are made up partly or entirely of court interpreters.

Countries where interpreters themselves have taken the initiative in setting standards tend to have active professional organizations. In Canada, for example, the Society of Translators and Interpreters of British Colombia (STIBC) developed a certification exam in the early 1980s that was eventually adopted for the entire country and is now overseen by the Canadian Translators and Interpreters Council (CTIC). In the United Kingdom, a similar situation prevails: The Institute of Translators and Interpreters (ITI), which represents court, business, and conference interpreters, administers proficiency exams in various fields of specialization. It awards the Diploma in Public Service Interpreting, which can be taken in four specialized options: English legal, Scottish legal, health, and local government services (Corsellis 1995). The Australian Institute of Interpreters and Translators (AUSIT) works closely with the national accreditation organization in encouraging interpreters to hone their skills and obtain their professional credentials. All of these organizations hold regular conferences and training sessions for the benefit of their members and engage in efforts to educate the public about their profession.

Until relatively recently, court interpreting was ignored by the established schools for interpreters. What little training was available was offered by professional associations. European schools of conference interpreting may have a course in legal interpreting as part of their curriculum, but none offers degrees or specializations in judiciary interpreting. Sweden, always in the vanguard, first developed training programs for community interpreters (including court interpreters) in folk high schools in 1968; later on, more comprehensive interpreter training was introduced at the university level (Ozolins 1998). In the United States, the Monterey Institute of International Studies offered its first certificate course in court interpreting in 1983 as an adjunct to the Master of Arts (graduate degree) in Conference Interpreting. That same year, the University of Arizona began its yearly Summer Institute of Court Interpretation. Since that time, universities and colleges all over the United States have launched certificate courses in court interpreting. The first school to offer a degree in the field was the University of Charleston, South Carolina, which began its M.A. in Legal Interpreting and Translating in 1996. California State University at Long Beach is in the process of developing a Bachelor of Arts (undergraduate) programme in interpreting (Burris 1999), and other universities will undoubtedly follow suit.

In Australia, the first training courses for interpreters were offered in the mid 1970s, and more were developed as the national accreditation programme took shape (Ozolins 1998). The National Accreditation Authority for Translators and Interpreters (NAATI) approves and oversees training courses, and because the training is directly geared to the accreditation exams, which do not test subspecialties, court interpreting is taught incidentally rather than as a separate field of specialization. In Canada, Vancouver Community College has had a programme in court interpreting since 1979 (González et al 1991), and other colleges and universities have begun offering training in this type of interpreting for both indigenous-language speakers and speakers of the major languages of immigration (Sammons 1993; Roberts 1997). In the United

Kingdom, more than 20 colleges now offer courses designed to help interpreters prepare for the Diploma in Public Service Interpreting, which includes a legal specialization (Corsellis 1995).

A complicating factor in efforts to raise standards and regulate the court interpreting profession is the multiplicity of languages involved. Whereas conference interpreting is limited to the major languages of international diplomacy and business, and thus can focus training efforts on those languages, virtually any language in the world may be required in a court proceeding. The relative ease of travel and rapid communication, the globalization of trade, as well as ethnic strife and international border disputes, have all resulted in record levels of international migration and court cases involving multiple languages. Some jurisdictions have fairly stable immigrant populations and predictable language needs, while others face the challenge of constant demographic changes. It is extremely difficult to maintain uniform standards for interpreters across languages in any case, and when the languages of greatest need are always in flux, it is almost impossible to keep up with the required training and monitoring of court interpreters.

The adoption of high standards by legislatures, courts, and professional associations and the emergence of specialized training programs for court interpreters mean increasing recognition of court interpreting as a viable profession and a career choice for talented bilinguals. It remains to be seen over the coming decades whether interpreters in the judiciary will enjoy working conditions and professional respect commensurate with the extensive preparation and commitment required to achieve proficiency.

Suggestions for Further Reading

Carr, Silvana, Roda Roberts, Aileen Dufour and Dini Steyn (eds) (1997) *The Critical Link: Interpreters in the Community*, Amsterdam & Philadelphia: John Benjamins.

Colin, Joan and Ruth Morris (1996) *Interpreters and the Legal Process*, Winchester: Waterside Press.

Corsellis, Ann (1995) *Non-English Speakers and the English Legal System*, Cambridge: The Institute of Criminology, University of Cambridge, Cropwood Occasional Paper No. 20.

Gaiba, Francesca (1998) *The Origins of Simultaneous Interpretation: The Nuremberg Trial*, Ottawa: University of Ottawa Press.

González, Roseann, Victoria Vásquez and Holly Mikkelson (1991) *Fundamentals of Court Interpretation: Theory, Policy and Practice*, Durham, North Carolina: Carolina Academic Press.

Katschinka, Liese and Christine Springer (eds) (1999) *Proceedings of the Fourth International Forum and First European Congress on Court Interpreting and*

Legal Translation "Language Is a Human Right", Vienna: Fédération Internationale des Traducteurs.

Moeketsi, Rosemary (1999a) *Discourse in a Multilingual and Multicultural Courtroom: A Court Interpreter's Guide*, Pretoria: JL van Schaik.

Roberts, Roda (ed) (1981) *L'interprétation auprès des tribunaux*, Ottawa: Editions de l'Université d'Ottawa.

Ozolins, Uldis (1998) *Interpreting & Translating in Australia: Current Issues and International Comparisons*, Victoria: The National Languages and Literacy Institute of Australia).

2. The Law

> Beyond legal arguments, it is a fair and just presumption that in court a person should be allowed to understand the proceedings and be given the opportunity to communicate in his or her preferred mode of discourse, or be provided with an intermediary who can facilitate that communication.
>
> González et al (1991:49)

Interpreters fulfill a variety of functions in the legal sphere: They assist law enforcement agencies in questioning witnesses and suspects, enable attorneys to communicate with their clients, interpret court proceedings for defendants and litigants, and interpret witness testimony for the court. The interpreter may be regarded as an arm of the law, part of the defence or prosecution "team", an expert witness, or an impartial officer of the court. In this chapter we will examine the laws and regulations that govern court interpreting, legal definitions of what constitutes a competent interpreter, and credentialing requirements for court interpreters in various countries.

The Right to an Interpreter

When an official agency or institution such as the police, the public prosecutor, or a court requires the services of an interpreter to assist in investigating a crime or examining a witness, there is never any doubt of its legal authority to obtain those services. The code of criminal procedure may contain some provisions about interpreters as expert witnesses or evidence obtained through an interpreter, but the presence of the interpreter is not a controversial issue. The potential for abuse, and hence the controversy, arises when an individual who does not speak the language of the court is accused of a crime. Because the language barrier prevents that individual from defending himself properly, and because unscrupulous authorities may not consider it to be in their best interests to provide an interpreter for the defendant, special safeguards are required to protect individual rights and guarantee due process. That is why the United Nations International Covenant on Civil and Political Rights of 1966 provides, in Article 14,

> 3. In the determination of any criminal charge against him, everyone shall be entitled to the following minimum guarantees, in full equality:
> a. To be informed promptly and in detail in a language which he understands of the nature and cause of the charge against him;

b. To have adequate time and facilities for the preparation of his defence and to communicate with counsel of his own choosing; ...

f. To have the free assistance of an interpreter if he cannot understand or speak the language used in court; ... (Ishay 1997:429)

Europe

In Europe, virtually all countries guarantee the right to an interpreter for litigants who do not speak the language of the proceedings. The Convention for the Protection of Human Rights and Fundamental Freedoms, adopted by the Council of Europe in 1950, guarantees in Article 6, among other things, 1) that the defendant in a criminal case be present in person when the case is heard in court, 2) that the evidence be heard by an "impartial tribunal", and 3) that the defendant be informed of the charges "in a language which he understands" and shall "have the free assistance of an interpreter if he cannot understand or speak the language used in the court" (Jacobs and White 1996:122-123).

Many European countries also have separate provisions in their constitutions or statutes guaranteeing the right to an interpreter. In the Czech Republic, for example, the relevant law is Act No. 36 of 1967; in Poland, it is the Law on the System of Common Courts of 1985; in Denmark, the Danish Administration of Justice Act. In Greece and Italy it is the Code of Criminal Procedure that requires the presence of an interpreter for foreign litigants. Often the guarantees are not backed up by practical mechanisms, however. For example, Gourevitch (1997) points out that while Russian law states that citizens have the right to conduct legal affairs in their mother tongue, the code of criminal procedure contains no provision for interpreters.

In Sweden, the right to an interpreter is established in the Code of Judicial Procedure, the Administrative Procedures Act, and the State Officials Act. Community interpreting, which includes the subspecialty of court interpreting, has long been recognized as a profession in Sweden, and Stockholm University's Institute for Interpretation and Translation Studies oversees training courses throughout the country. After undergoing this training, candidates take an exam administered by a national judicial board to become authorized interpreters (Colin and Morris 1996).

Ozolins (1998:115) points out that despite their formidable traditions in translation and interpretation, German-speaking countries "were among the least responsive in Europe to the multilingual population that moved there from the 1960s to power the economic miracles", and that

> attitudes to non-German speakers were at best cool, with language inadequacies clearly blamed on the non-German speakers themselves. Communication with institutions was done on a completely ad hoc

basis, with the tradition of bring-your-own interpreter continuing to the present day.

Pöchhacker (1997:218) notes that although Austria has had an association of court interpreters since 1920,

> a sound legal basis for the exercise of court interpreting was established only in 1975, and it was not until the early 1980s that an examination was introduced to test the would-be practitioners' translating and interpreting skills and familiarity with the legal subject-matter and technical terminology before a panel of legal experts and interpreters. This has now become a standard requirement for inclusion in the register of generally sworn interpreters. It must be pointed out, however, that there is still no formalized training module or complementary course in court interpreting as such in Austria's three university departments for translator and interpreter training.

In the United Kingdom, the only common-law jurisdiction in Europe, "arrangements concerning the provision of interpreters in the legal system are essentially still haphazard" (Corsellis 1995). The Royal Commission on Criminal Justice has made recommendations on developing a system for providing interpreting services in the courts, but no laws have been enacted yet. Because the common law relies on precedent decisions, the courts themselves are gradually establishing the legal principles governing court interpreting in cases such as *R. v. Iqbal Begun* of 1991. In addition, the Police and Criminal Evidence Act (PACE) of 1984 contains guidelines for criminal investigations involving non-English-speakers (Corsellis 1995; Colin and Morris 1996).

The Americas

In the United States, interpreters are considered an essential element in guaranteeing the defendant's right to due process under the Fifth and Sixth Amendments to the Constitution. The interpreter protects those rights primarily by ensuring the defendant's "presence" when his case is heard, providing a complete simultaneous interpretation of everything that is said in court. The defendant's right to be present at all stages of the proceedings has long been recognized in U.S. case law (*Lewis v. United States* 1892), and the notion of "linguistic presence" (i.e., that the defendant cannot be present at his trial if he does not understand the language of the proceedings) was established in *Arizona v. Natividad* (1974). A California case, *People v. Chavez* (1981), declared that appointing a bilingual defence attorney is not enough to guarantee a defendant's right to interpretation. The Court Interpreters Act of 1978 established a certification programme to ensure the competency of interpreters working in the federal courts, and numerous states have enacted laws or regulations concerning the quality of interpreting in the state courts.

Canada, also a common-law country, provides similar guarantees. The Canadian Charter of Rights and Freedoms of 1982 states in Section 14 that "a party or witness in any proceeding who does not understand or speak the language in which the proceedings are conducted or who is deaf has the right of the assistance of an interpreter" (Northwest Territories Justice 1993:1-2). With its large population of indigenous groups, Canada has made special provisions for interpreters in aboriginal languages (Repa 1988; Akeeshoo 1993).

The American Convention on Human Rights, signed in 1969 and adopted in 1978 as an Organization of American States treaty, recognizes in Article 8, Paragraph 2 (a) "the right of the accused to be assisted without charge by a translator or interpreter, if he does not understand or does not speak the language of the tribunal or court". Individual countries in Latin America have their own provisions for meeting the language needs of litigants who do not speak the language of the courts. Argentina, for example, has a well-established public translator profession, with highly respected university degree programmes in translation and strict regulations governing practice. Given that until recently most legal proceedings were conducted in writing, public translators were able to meet the courts' language needs quite effectively, and only rarely would interpretation of oral testimony be required. With the recent advent of oral trials, however, this situation has changed, and the profession has had to adopt new guidelines to incorporate the additional interpretation duties (Colegio de Traductores Públicos 1997). Brazilian public translators are also required to be prepared to interpret in court when called upon to do so (Randmer 1998).

Other Latin American countries have taken steps to acknowledge the rights of linguistic minorities who appear in court. In Mexico, for example, while there is no constitutional guarantee of the right to an interpreter, the Code of Criminal Procedure allows the judge to appoint an interpreter if any defendant, complainant, witness, or expert does not speak enough Spanish to communicate effectively. In the case of a non-Spanish-speaking defendant, a 1991 revision of the Federal Code of Criminal Procedure specifies that the interpreter is to be appointed as soon as the arrest takes place, and is to be made available throughout the proceedings to enable the defendant to communicate with counsel (Colín Sánchez 1992).

Countries with large aboriginal populations have only recently made provisions for interpretation in indigenous languages. According to Weller Ford (1992), between 55 and 60 indigenous languages are still spoken in Mexico, and efforts are now being made to train interpreters to meet the needs of monolingual Indians in their dealings with Mexican public agencies. In Guatemala, the peace accord of 1994 acknowledged the rights of indigenous Guatemalans and contained provisions for translation and interpretation services (Landaverde 1999).

Asia

Although many Asian countries are signatories to agreements such as the International Covenant on Civil and Political Rights of 1966, they do not necessarily adhere to all of the provisions of these treaties. For example, according to Tsuda (1997:22), Japan's courts routinely violate this covenant:

> The problems facing foreigners suspected of involvement in crimes are numerous, the most basic of which are the lack of knowledge of Japan's criminal procedures, and a low level of comprehension of the Japanese language. Foreigners find themselves in a state of utter helplessness as they are interrogated by police officers who equally do not understand the foreign language and culture. Foreigners have a great difficulty distinguishing between police officers and prosecutors and more often than not, are left ill-advised by their own defence counsels, who similarly have communication problems with their foreign clients.

In contrast, interpreters have long been a fixture in the courts of Malaysia, a land of many ethnic groups, cultures, and languages. Indeed, Khoon (1990:109) asserts, "It is a fact that almost every case that comes to the courts, be it civil or criminal, requires the help of an interpreter". The Malaysian code of criminal procedure states, "Whenever any evidence is given in a language not understood by the accused, and he is present in person it shall be interpreted to him in open court in a language which he understands" (Cap. 6 270 [1], quoted in Khoon 1990). Another Asian country with a long multilingual tradition is Singapore, where court interpreting has been given high priority. An innovative system of remote interpreting using video conferencing allows a centralized corps of interpreters to serve courts located anywhere in the country (Ozolins 1998). Hong Kong also developed a sophisticated court interpreting system under British rule, when court proceedings were conducted in English. It remains to be seen whether minority languages will be acknowledged by the Chinese authorities, and whether the tradition of quality interpreting in the courts will be maintained.

Elsewhere in Asia, and in the Middle East, Ozolins (1998:116) laments that "often quite radical multilingualism can exist without much concern for providing language services". Even in India, with nine official languages, little interpreting takes place in public agencies, he reports. In the Middle East, "now a region of massive international labour movement, ... there is little likelihood that language services of any kind would develop for these internal needs". And in Israel, he reports, "the time-honoured response of trusting to ubiquitous multilingual individuals to broker language situations is continuing", despite the presence of highly trained interpreters who have written extensively about legal interpreting. Bell (1997) notes that many practitioners in Hong Kong, Indonesia, and Japan, lacking any accreditation in their own country, have taken Australia's exam to enhance their credentials. There is a possibility of offering the examinations to interpreters in Taiwan, Korea, and China as well, Bell indicates.

Australia

Like the United Kingdom and Canada, Australia does not have a constitutional or statutory guarantee of the right to an interpreter, but precedent decisions and rules of court address the needs of non-English-speaking litigants. For example, the ruling in *R. v. Lee Kun* stated that an accused cannot be present at his trial if he does not understand the language of the court (Gentile et al 1996). As Ozolins (1998:9) points out, in countries where constitutional guarantees of the sort seen in the United States are "muted or nonexistent, there has been no explicit prioritizing of court interpreting over language services for other areas of public life". Rather, generic language services have been set up to meet the various needs of the public sector, and standards have been developed in an ad hoc but effective manner, according to Ozolins. Until recently, aboriginal languages were treated differently from the languages of immigrants, but efforts are now being made to integrate them into other language service structures (Ozolins 1998). Specific provision is made for interpreting aboriginal languages in Article 5 of the Convention on the Elimination of All Forms of Racism (Cooke 1995).

Africa

Many African countries are struggling to keep up with the rest of the world in the area of civil rights. It is interesting to note that the African Charter on Human and Peoples' Rights of 1986, which is largely patterned after the International Covenant on Civil and Political Rights of 1966 and contains wording very similar to that of the European Convention for the Protection of Human Rights and Fundamental Freedoms and the American Convention on Human Rights, does not contain any provision for court interpreters (Ishay 1997). Some African countries with long multilingual traditions do have laws requiring the presence of interpreters in court proceedings, however.

South Africa had two official languages under the apartheid system, thus setting a precedent for interpreting in the courts. The formal training of court interpreters dates back to 1957 (Ozolins 1998), and now encompasses all the major languages of the country. South Africa is making an effort to guarantee high standards for interpreting in all of its 11 official languages (Inggs 1998; Moeketsi 1999a & b). Today every citizen has a right to demand a trial in his own language, which means that English- or Afrikaans-speaking judges (who are still in the majority on the bench) must depend totally on interpreters to understand the proceedings (Moeketsi 1999b:13). Indeed, Moeketsi asserts that "it is solely through [the interpreter's] language proficiency and his familiarity with the cultures of the defendant and that of the courtroom that the court can even think of proceeding".

The proceedings of the Truth and Reconciliation Commission, which began in 1995 as South Africa made the transition to democracy, provided a valuable experience in conducting multilingual hearings with simultaneous interpretation (Kingscott 1997). It is also significant that interpreters have had a major presence in the war crimes trials in Rwanda; perhaps that experience will have a positive influence on the development of the profession in neighbouring countries (International Criminal Tribunal for Rwanda 2000).

Defining Competence

It is one thing to enact a law requiring that an interpreter be present to assist litigants who do not speak the language of the court; it is quite another to determine whether that interpreter is competent, or to enable judiciary personnel to identify qualified interpreters. In most countries, unfortunately, decisions about whether an interpreter is required and who is qualified to act as an interpreter are left to the discretion of the judge. Judges are experts in the law, however, not in language or interpreting competence. In countries with well developed court interpreting programs, it has been found that an objective testing and credentialing system is the best way to eliminate subjective decision-making by identifying the most qualified court interpreters and making their names available to the judiciary.

U.S. Federal Court Interpreters Exam

Perhaps the most widely respected exam designed to test court interpreter proficiency is the Federal Court Interpreter Certification Exam developed for the United States Administrative Office of the Courts (González et al 1991). First administered in 1980 and given regularly since then, the exam consists of two parts. Candidates first take a written exam that tests their knowledge of the formal registers of English and the second language (at present the test is given in Spanish, Navajo, and Haitian-Creole) at the college level of comprehension. Subsections include reading comprehension, synonyms, sentence completion, usage, and antonyms, for a total of 160 multiple-choice questions, 80 in each language (González et al 1991:525).

Candidates who pass the written test qualify to take the oral portion, a 45-minute exam in which they must demonstrate their proficiency in sight translation, simultaneous interpreting, and consecutive interpreting. The sight translation section consists of two 250-word texts on law-related subjects, one in English and the other in the second language, each of which they must translate orally in five minutes. The simultaneous component has two subsections, one an attorney's argument recorded at approximately 120 words per minute, and the other a cross-examination at approximately 160 words per minute. The candidate is tested in simultaneous interpretation from English to the other language but not vice-versa, which reflects actual practice in the courtrooms of the United States. The consecutive interpreting segment consists of a 15-minute live simulation of an attorney's examination of a witness, with questions in English and answers in the other language. The candidate must interpret detailed statements up to 60 words in length without interrupting the speaker. All of the material to be interpreted is carefully selected to reflect actual courtroom language and situations (González et al 1991:527-529).

The written portion, being multiple-choice, is machine scored, whereas the oral portion is administered live before a panel of interpreters and language experts who have been trained to rate this particular exam. González et al (1991:529) describe the way the exam is scored:

> The unique feature of the oral examination is its bipartite rating system involving subjective and objective assessment ... Two hundred and twenty (220) objective scoring units, distributed throughout the examination, represent important interpreting pitfalls, such as commonly used legal phrases, specialized terminology, grammatical items, idiomatic expressions, jargon, rhetorically charged argumentative language, purposefully ambiguous or extremely precise language, dates, addresses, quantities, and exhibit numbers, among others.

Over the years since its inception, the pass rate for the two-part test has hovered around five percent (NCITRP 1999), a figure which reflects the rigorous standards set by the exam, the difficulty of court interpreting, and the lack of training programmes to help candidates prepare for it. Although the exam was challenged in court by an unsuccessful candidate, it was found to be a valid and reliable test of the skills required of interpreters in the courtroom (González et al 1991:524). To ensure its validity, the test developers first conducted a needs assessment, in which judges, interpreters, linguists, and psychometricians analyzed the tasks performed by court interpreters and determined the best way to test the prerequisite skills. Once the test instrument was written, it was piloted and subjected to statistical analyses. Each time a new instrument is developed, it is subjected to the same process to guarantee reliability and validity (González et al 1991:531-532).

The Federal Court Interpreter Certification Exam has been criticized as an expensive and elaborate test that leaves the courts without enough interpreters to meet their needs. Whether or not that criticism is fair, it is true that the high cost of administering the exam has limited the number of languages in which it can be given. Many state court systems have implemented more streamlined testing procedures that nevertheless attempt to test for the same qualities. Because they are less expensive to administer, these tests can be given more frequently and in more languages than the federal exam. One state, California, tests interpreters in eight languages and requires a test in English proficiency for interpreters in all other languages (Judicial Council of California 1998). There has been heated debate about the relative merits of the state and federal certification procedures, but objective testing has become an accepted standard for selecting court interpreters.

Other Exams

The Federal Court Interpreter Certification Exam has been used as a model for other jurisdictions in developing their exams for court interpreters, but it is not the only exemplar available. The Registry of Interpreters for the Deaf, also in the United States, has devised a highly respected exam to test the proficiency of sign-language interpreters, and it also contains a legal skills component. To be eligible to take the legal skills test, candidates must already be certified by the RID for general interpretation, and must show proof of formal legal training and experience in legal interpreting (RID 1995). They must then pass the written exam (which consists of 100 multiple-choice questions on language, the judicial system, team interpreting, and professional issues) to be eligible for the performance test. The latter is presented on videotape, and includes interpretation of various court proceedings and witness testimony, as well as a voir dire examination on interpreter qualifications (RID 1995:11-12).

Sweden has a well-developed system for ensuring quality interpretation that dates back to 1968 (Niska 1998). The National Agency of Lands and Funds administers accreditation tests of community interpreters, who are certified at a basic level and may obtain specialization in court or medical interpreting. The basic level test has a written component that serves as a prerequisite for the oral component, a performance exam that also covers professional ethics and interpreting technique. Norway has recently implemented a Public Service Interpreter Certification Examination similar to Sweden's, but it combines health care and legal interpreting in a single exam. Candidates take a five-hour written exam on terminology, language usage, and factual knowledge, and an oral exam lasting one-and-a-half to two hours, in which candidates interpret simulated dialogues and answer questions about interpreting techniques and professional ethics (University of Oslo 1996).

The Australian certification programme is another model worthy of study. Rather than focusing on specific types of interpreting, Australia has a multi-tiered programme of accreditation in which interpreters are rated at four different levels: 1) Paraprofessional Interpreter, 2) Interpreter, 3) Conference Interpreter, and 4) Conference Interpreter (Senior). This generalist approach is unique in that it allows all interpreters to strive for the highest level of certification, regardless of what setting they work in. In other words, court interpreters are not automatically regarded as inferior to conference interpreters, as is the case in many countries. Ozolins (1998:42) explains that the designers of the accreditation system wanted to avoid

> an exclusive demarcation between the previously established profession of conference interpreters and technical translators for international needs on the one hand, and the newer emerging group of interpreters and translators servicing local needs on the other; rather, they saw all these practitioners as essentially the one profession with differences of specialities and levels as in other professions.

Candidates for Level 2, Interpreter, are tested in consecutive interpreting only, whereas candidates for the higher levels are tested in both consecutive and simultaneous interpreting (Bell 1997). It is recommended, though not required by law, that court proceedings be interpreted by interpreters at the third level or above. The test is now given in over 50 languages (Ozolins 1998).

In the United Kingdom, the National Register of Public Service Interpreters was established in 1994 (Corsellis 1995). To be fully registered, an interpreter must have a recognized qualification in public service interpreting and evidence of appropriate work experience. The Diploma in Public Service Interpreting is such a qualification, and it can be obtained by taking an accredited course of study or by sitting for the Public Service Interpreting Exam administered by the Institute of Translators and Interpreters (ITI). The exam includes two interpreting role plays and translation in both directions (Corsellis 1997). Despite the lack of legislation requiring the use of registered Public Service Interpreters, the ITI is striving to ensure that courts throughout the United Kingdom implement such regulations (Tybulewicz 1997).

In Canada, the certification exam for court interpreters is overseen by the Canadian Translators and Interpreters Council (CTIC). Candidates are tested in language proficiency, legal terminology and procedures, consecutive interpreting, and a mock trial. Moeketsi (1999a) reports that in South Africa, where it is common for court interpreters to have as many as six or seven working languages, candidates are given several written passages to translate to and from their languages, and must answer a series of questions about the legal system. Those who pass this test receive a two-day orientation and on-the-job training with gradually decreasing supervision by a mentor. At some point after they begin working, they are sent to Justice College Pretoria for six weeks of training in criminal and civil procedure, legal terminology, translation theory, and interpreting techniques. There is no final exam to determine whether they have mastered the skills presented in this training; the interpreters are simply sent back to the courts where they have been working.

It is clear from this discussion that the selection of interpreters is too crucial a decision to be left to judges and lawyers, or self-reporting of individuals who place their name on a list, as is done in many countries (Martonova 1997; Manganaras 1997). Countries with the most highly developed court interpreting programmes have found that objective performance exams are the best way to identify individuals with the skills required to carry out this important task.

The Role of the Professional Association

The professional association plays a critical role in establishing and maintaining high standards of performance in court interpreting. In some countries, interpreting exams are administered by the associations themselves (as is the case in Canada and the U.K.), while in others (e.g., Australia and the U.S.), professional associations work closely with government agencies and accrediting bodies to guarantee the quality of testing programmes. In addition to providing services for their members, such as training, dissemination of news, liaison with the judicial system, and advocating for the profession, these organizations also strive to educate the public about language issues in general and court interpreting in particular, and teach other professionals how to work effectively with interpreters.

Suggestions for Further Study

1. Discuss why it is important to have a competent interpreter, and what problems could arise without one. Do you think the government should provide interpreters free of charge for everyone who needs one? Is competent interpreting equally important in criminal and civil cases? Why or why not?

2. Find out what laws and regulations govern court interpreting in your country. How do they compare to those discussed in this chapter? If you could write a law on court interpreting, what would it say?

3. Find out if there is a professional organization of interpreters in your country. If so, what are its functions, and who are its members? If not, discuss with your class how you might go about forming such an asso-

ciation. Decide what you want the organization to be like, and draft by-laws for it.

4. Identify the characteristics you think a court interpreter should have, and outline an exam that tests for those qualities. Decide whether you would have written or oral components, and give reasons for your decision.

3. Legal Traditions of the World

> We see neither justice nor injustice which does not change its nature
> with change in climate. Three degrees of latitude reverse all juris-
> prudence; a meridian decides the truth.
> > Blaise Pascal (1670; in *International Thesaurus*
> > *of Quotations* 1996:352)

> There is something monstrous in commands couched in invented and
> unfamiliar language; an alien master is the worst of all. The language of
> the law must not be foreign to the ears of those who are to obey it.
> > Learned Hand (1929; in *International Thesaurus*
> > *of Quotations* 1996:367)

The role played by the interpreter in the different phases of litigation is a function of the legal system prevailing in the country in question, and of the specific
laws and regulations governing interpreted proceedings. In this chapter we will
examine the major legal traditions of the world, the influence they have on each
other, and the way they affect people's daily lives.

Attitudes Towards the Law and Lawyers

Every society has rules of behaviour and mechanisms for judging and punish-
ing those who violate the rules, and for resolving disputes between individuals.
The more sophisticated the society, the more complex the mechanisms. Human
affairs have become so complicated that it takes specialists to navigate the elaborate systems that have been devised to promulgate laws, enforce them, interpret
them, and serve as advocates for the individuals who are affected by them. Unfortunately for the hapless laypersons caught up in the justice system, it is not
always easy to understand the language and behaviour of professionals who
spend their entire working lives immersed in the complexities of the law. As a
result, the general public feels alienated and mistrustful. Lawyers, in particular,
are viewed with suspicion by those who are dependent on them to make sense
out of the arcane and sometimes bizarre workings of the judicial system. The
number of derogatory terms for lawyers is evidence of the contempt in which
they are held: in English, *shyster, pettifogger, ambulance chaser, mouthpiece,
shark*; in Spanish, *buscapleitos, leguleyo, picapleitos, rábula, tinterillo, abogado
firmón*; in French, *avocassier, chicaneur, avocat marron*, and so on. Mistrust
of lawyers is not just a Western phenomenon; Leng and Chiu (1985:94) report
that the Chinese consider lawyers "troublemaking and even traitorous", and
Tanaka (1976:265) notes that traditionally in Japan,

> ... practicing attorneys were looked upon as intruders, meddling unin-
> vited in disputes which otherwise could have been resolved in the
> traditional spirit of "harmony". Even in criminal cases, a practicing at-
> torney was viewed not as an agent charged with the grave responsibility
> of protecting the civil rights of the accused but as an apologist begging
> for mercy, or even worse, as a schemer bent on thwarting the law.

One reason for this animosity, of course, is the fact that people usually come
into contact with lawyers and the courts only when they are accused of a crime,
are the victim of a crime, or are engaged in a dispute with someone – never a
pleasant experience. Another reason is the reputation lawyers have earned for
obfuscation. Most societies' legal systems are closely related to their religious
traditions, and both are the product of centuries of cultural and moral evolution.
The language of the law is thus steeped in tradition, full of archaic expressions,
weighed down by scholarly reasoning, and shackled with deeply entrenched
formulas that no one dares to change. Legal reforms often include efforts to
simplify the language of legislation and legal documents, as evidenced by the
"plain English" movements in the United States and the United Kingdom. Even
in China, Maoist reformers ordered that all court documents be written in "colloquial simple language" rather than the traditional legal style (Ladany 1992:57).

Despite these efforts, legal professionals still seem to be out of touch with
the ordinary people who must do business with the courts, however unwill-
ingly. The barriers that already exist between the average citizen and the legal
system become even greater when that person does not share the predominant
language and culture of the country in question. In these circumstances, as a
court interpreter you will have to bridge the gap not only between languages
and cultures, but also between legal traditions. For this reason, you should have
some familiarity with comparative legal systems. Every country in the world
has its own way of establishing and enforcing rules of behaviour for its citizens.
Scholars have identified many common features within that diversity, and have
classified the world's legal systems into two main traditions, civil law and common law.

Civil Law

The civil-law tradition can be traced back to the *Corpus Juris Civilis* of the
Roman Empire, beginning with the publication of the XII Tables in Rome in
450 B.C. For that reason, the term **Roman law** is often used for this tradition as
well. When later European empires established colonies throughout the world,
they created institutions that survived even after the colonies gained their inde-
pendence. Consequently, civil law today prevails not only in Europe, but also in
Central and South America and much of Asia and Africa. It is also found in

enclaves of the common-law world (Louisiana, Puerto Rico, and Quebec, for example). In addition, the Western European experts who developed the principles of international law and designed the international courts of the League of Nations, the United Nations, the European Union, and other multinational organizations, were heavily influenced by the civil-law tradition. (Important note: The term **civil law** is used not only to identify the legal tradition discussed here, but also to denote the litigation of private rights and remedies, in contrast to **penal** or **criminal law**.)

The fall of Rome in the fifth century A.D. did not mark the end of the influence of Roman law on Europeans. During the Middle Ages, Germanic invaders spread Roman legal concepts, colored by their own traditions and customary law, among the peoples of Europe. Christian canon law also influenced the development of European legal systems. During the period known as the Enlightenment in the eighteenth century, philosophers further refined the concepts embodied in the Romano-Germanic tradition and established the principles that now form the basis of the world's legal systems. These principles have become so indelibly etched in human consciousness that they are now taken for granted, but in the eighteenth century they were considered revolutionary. Among these concepts is the **rule of law**, that is, the notion that a society's rules should be written down and enforced consistently for everyone, rather than being subject to the whims of whoever is in power at the moment. It stems from the parallel theses *nullum crimen sine lege* (no crime without a law) and *nullum poena sine lege* (no penalty without a law), which were first expressed by Cesare Beccaria in his 1764 work *Of Crimes and Punishments*. Throughout Europe, newly emerging nations began drawing up written laws, or **codes**, that incorporated the political and philosophical ideas of the time.

On the other hand, eighteenth century philosophers also built on the Roman concept of *jus naturale* (**natural law**), which postulated that certain rules of behaviour derived from human nature could be identified as universals, independent of the enacted laws of any one nation (known as **positive law**). These scholars explored the conflicts that might arise between what the law says and what is inherently right or just. The French and American Revolutions were inspired by the theory that mankind has certain inherent rights that transcend the laws of regimes in power.

The civil-law tradition's approach to crime and punishment represented the culmination of efforts to move away from private vengeance by establishing that public officials rather than individuals would be the accusers, thereby relieving the victim of the responsibility of pursuing the offender, and placing the power of the government behind the quest for justice. In addition, the judge, an independent professional, was given the authority to gather evidence (both against and in favour of the accused) and to control the nature and objectives of the inquiry in secret proceedings, secrecy being considered necessary to protect victims from powerful individuals whom they accused of crimes. Because these inquisitorial powers were often abused, subsequent legal reforms lifted the veil of secrecy and gave the accused more participation in the proceedings. Nevertheless, in civil-law systems, the judge remains a central figure in the investigation of crimes and the presentation of evidence in private disputes.

Two codes in particular, the French Civil Code of 1804 and the German Civil Code of 1896, had a great impact on legal thought not only in Europe, but throughout the world. According to Glendon et al (1996:41-42),

> Both were grounded in nineteenth century European-style liberalism. That is, they were infused with then current notions of individual autonomy, freedom of contract and private property. But over the course of the near-century that separated the two codes, society had been changing profoundly. Industrialization and much social unrest had intervened. Thus, while the German Civil Code still resembled the French in its solicitude for private property, freedom of contract and the traditional family, it also reflected a number of new developments that had occurred since 1804.

The French code was written in simple terms so that the average person could understand it, whereas the German code was a highly complex codification of legal concepts accessible only to trained experts. Though they differ from each other in approach, each has contributed key elements to modern legal systems all over the world. French revolutionary ideas and German legal science are considered "the two principal tributaries to the modern civil law tradition" (Glendon et al 1996:44).

The most distinguishing features of the civil-law tradition, then, are that all laws are written down in codes that impose strict rules of procedure and guidelines to ensure uniform and predictable outcomes; and that within the limits of those guidelines, judges exercise a great deal of control over the litigation, though they are limited to applying the provisions of the codes and do not become a source of law themselves.

Common Law

The common-law tradition traces its roots to 1066, when the Normans invaded the island of Britain, and was developed primarily in England. It came to be called **common** because in the Middle Ages, law was a local phenomenon, and in the twelfth century King Henry II for the first time instituted a system that was common to all parts of his realm. Common law is also known as **unwritten law**, because originally it was a body of customary law based on judicial decisions rather than codes or statutes. To this day, England has no written constitution, though of course it has as many written laws as any other country. Other common-law countries do have written constitutions, however, because when the legal system was exported to British colonies in the eighteenth and nineteenth centuries, new elements were incorporated in keeping with current trends. Today the common-law tradition is predominant in the legal systems of the United Kingdom, Ireland, the United States, Canada, Australia, and New Zealand, and it also has a major influence in the former British colonies of Asia and Africa.

Common law is also sometimes known as **judge-made law**, because it adheres to the principle of *stare decisis* (the decision stands), meaning that judges are bound to follow the decisions made by other judges in similar cases. Judicial decisions are important sources of law in other systems as well, but there they tend to be advisory rather than mandatory. Another unique feature of common law (though it has now been adopted and adapted for criminal cases in many countries) is the lay jury. In contrast to the civil-law tradition, in which a judge or panel of judges decides cases, in the common law, it is a jury of ordinary citizens that issues the verdict. Critics of common law say that it is much less predictable, and therefore more capricious and subjective, than civil law because judges are given the power to interpret the law, and because ordinary citizens untrained in the law (and therefore subject to being swayed by canny lawyers) are given the final say with respect to guilt or innocence. The counter-argument is that involving citizens in the legal system ensures against abuse by legal professionals who are not answerable to the public and can easily lose touch with the man in the street.

Merryman and Clark (1978) identify three other predominant elements that characterize common-law proceedings: 1) **concentration**, meaning that all evidence is presented in a single event, the trial; 2) **immediacy**, in that the judge actually sees and hears evidence first-hand, rather than reading reports and affidavits; and 3) **orality**, referring to the fact that witness testimony is given live in public proceedings. There is an increasing trend in civil-law countries toward adopting these features as well, however. For example, Germany has undergone major reforms recently that make its criminal proceedings much more similar to the common-law model (Huber 1996).

Another oft-mentioned aspect of the common-law tradition is that it is **accusatorial**, as opposed to the **inquisitorial** approach taken under civil law. In an accusatorial system, the trial is a contest between two equal sides who try to persuade a neutral referee (consisting of the judge, who enforces the rules of procedure, and the jury, which decides on the facts) to rule in their favour. As noted earlier, in an inquisitorial system, the judge plays an active role in the fact-finding stage prior to reaching a decision, though the judge involved in the investigative stage is not the same one who issues the final judgement. Anthropologists consider the accusatorial approach to be the first substitute for private vengeance in an evolving society, as the right of accusation extends from the wronged individual to his family, his clan, and the entire society. In the modern form of accusatorial justice, the wronged party is represented by the public prosecutor, who uses the powers of the state (i.e., law enforcement agencies) to investigate the offence. The inquisitorial system is seen as a further step away from private vengeance because it is more impersonal (Merryman and Clark 1978).

These distinctions are important for gaining some historical perspective on different legal systems, but Merryman and Clark (1978:694) point out that the law is becoming increasingly uniform throughout the world, particularly with regard to criminal procedure:

> In a sense it can be said that the evolution of criminal procedure in the last two centuries in the civil law world has been away from the extremes and abuses of the inquisitorial system, and that the evolution in the common law world during the same period has been away from the abuses and excesses of the accusatorial system. The two systems, in other words, are converging from different directions toward roughly equivalent mixed systems of criminal procedure.

Judicial systems represent an attempt to rationalize dispute resolution, and lawyers, who value reason, tend to adopt structures that appear to them to be the most reasonable. As a result, in procedural law, there is a "general tendency for the judicial systems of various countries to advance and to keep pace with one another, which results in the increase of universal elements" (Tanaka 1976:445-446). Yet within the general framework of legal systems, each country has a unique set of institutions that maintain elements of its particular cultural heritage. As Merryman and Clark (1978:3) emphasize, a legal tradition

> is not a set of rules of law about contracts, corporations, and crimes, although such rules will almost always be in some sense a reflection of that tradition. Rather it is a set of deeply rooted, historically conditioned attitudes about the nature of law, about the role of law in the society and the polity, about the proper organization and operation of a legal system, and about the way law is or should be made, applied, studied, perfected, and taught. The legal tradition relates the legal system to the culture of which it is a partial expression. It puts the legal system into cultural perspective.

Other Legal Traditions

Although most countries today have a combination of common-law and civil-law features, it is important to consider other factors such as geography, religion, and the economic system to understand their influence on current legal practices and attitudes towards the law.

Africa

The legal systems of African countries are shaped by three sources: indigenous traditions, European colonial powers, and Islam. Some nations have woven these threads into an integral structure, while others have parallel court systems dealing with different aspects of the law (penal vs. family matters, for example). In the latter countries, citizens may be able to choose whether they want their marriage, for example, to be governed by the rules of Islam, an indigenous tradition, or the civil courts.

Virtually all African countries now have modern codes covering penal, commercial, and administrative matters. In practice, however, the application of the law may be guided by certain indigenous traditions, including an emphasis on conciliation and arbitration rather than litigation, vicarious liability (meaning that the entire family, clan, or village is held responsible for the acts of an individual), acceptance of ancient practices such as polygamy, and recognition of the family or clan as a legal entity. Adei (1981:55) cautions against overemphasizing local differences and stresses the similarities between African legal systems and those of the rest of the world:

> Is there any "African law"? There is no rule or feature common to African customary law which is not, as far as I know, shared by the customary law of some non-African people. ... African laws therefore resemble each other; they also resemble the laws of non-African peoples. Not only is the brotherhood of Africans exemplified thereby, but – and this is never too trite to need restatement – the brotherhood of the whole human race. Man, wherever he is and whatever his race, tends to react in similar ways to similar circumstances.

Hinduism

Hindu law is based on *dharmasastra*, the science of righteousness, which is inextricably linked to personal, family, and social life for followers of the Hindu religion. It is observed by Hindus all over the world when dealing with matters of personal status (e.g., marriage, domestic relations, succession) and daily living (e.g., diet and dress). More than a theology, the Hindu tradition interweaves social, spiritual, and legal teachings, placing a heavy emphasis on group identity rather than individualism. In India, where 80% of the population is Hindu, the formal legal system governs penal, commercial, and administrative matters, but village justice often prevails at the local level. As a result, there is heavy emphasis on consensus-building and maintaining harmony rather than identifying winners and losers in a dispute. In addition, kinship and caste take precedence over other relationships, and some laws enacted by the government with respect to issues such as the age of marriage, divorce, women's rights, and discrimination against lower castes may be simply ignored (Derrett 1963; Rudolph and Rudolph 1967).

Islam

The law of Islam, the *Shariah*, provides rules of conduct for every aspect of Moslem life. According to Hassan (1981:95),

> ... the reformative principles of Islam are concerned with a system of directions for human welfare (seeking justice, good deeds, equality, human rights, and brotherhood and aimed at forbidding aggression and providing defence thereto), improving the status of the weaker sex and the weak, upholding the sanctity of private ownership, fulfilling contracts and outlawing deceit, and distinguishing the public and private rights in penal matters.

As with other religious doctrines, the tenets of Islam in modern times are usually applied only to personal matters, leaving matters of penal, commercial, and administrative law to secular government authorities. In countries with predominantly Moslem populations, however, Islam is far more influential in these spheres than other religions are in other countries. In fact, one country, Pakistan, owes its very existence to Islam, while Iran is currently governed by a regime in which clerics play a predominant role. At any rate, the legal precepts of Islam are very similar to those of civil and common law with respect to matters such as the ownership of property and the enforcement of contracts. There are some major differences in penal law, however. In Islamic states, murder is still considered a private offence punishable by the victim's family, for example, and women are not considered competent to testify as witnesses.

Judaism

Jewish law is observed by Jews all over the world in their personal lives for matters such as marriage, kinship, diet, and holy days. Although Jewish law has been in existence for over 3,000 years, only one country in the world, Israel, has a majority Jewish population. Even in Israel, religious law applies only to questions of personal status and to claims brought voluntarily to rabbinical courts for arbitration. The law and lawyers are held in high esteem in Jewish culture, perhaps far more than in any other.

Socialist Law

The socialist legal tradition dates back to the 1918 October Revolution in Russia. The Soviets imposed certain principles of socialist ideology, such as the dictatorship of the proletariat and the abolition of private property, on existing systems that belonged to the civil-law family. At one time, socialist law prevailed throughout Eastern Europe and parts of Asia, Africa, and Latin America, but since the collapse of the Soviet Union and the legal reforms that have taken place in the former Soviet satellites, socialist law has been limited to a few isolated countries: Cuba, North Korea, Vietnam, and China. Each of these countries applies socialist law in a manner consistent with older legal and cultural traditions.

In Asian countries, ancient Confucianist principles still hold sway, though the communists have tried to give priority to socialist ideals and eradicate practices they consider decadent. Mao, in particular, was very distrustful of the law and the legal system, asserting that law was the "weapon of the dictatorship" (Ladany 1992:54), referring to both the system he overthrew and his own regime. Unlike the Soviets, Mao rejected almost every element of the legal institutions that were in place when he took over, although subsequent reforms have restored some of them. Still, Article 2 of the current Criminal Law of the People's Republic of China states that the purpose of the Chinese legal system is to protect first the socialist order, and second, individual rights. Some elements of the traditional Chinese system were retained in modified form, however. For example, according to Ladany (1992:71), during dynastic times, the nobility was considered exempt from punishment under the law, whereas in Maoist China, members of the Communist Party enjoyed a similar privilege (a distinction was made between those who were "within the People" i.e., with the party, and those who were not). China's system has been described as "the Chinese variety of socialist justice system with the blending of both Soviet and indigenous experiences. Western influences are also quite evident" (Leng and Chiu 1985:170).

Confucianism

The philosophy and teachings of Confucius date back to the fifth century B.C., yet they are still observed throughout East and Southeast Asia. Ladany (1992:1-2) contends that despite numerous upheavals in Chinese history, for 2,000 years the Chinese people enjoyed cultural continuity thanks to a "stable system of laws that remained fundamentally unchanged". Some concepts that were developed in traditional Confucian law, such as negligence, cumulative offences, and consideration of the defendant's personal background when imposing criminal sentences, are now accepted throughout the world. Confucianism, like many other traditional belief systems, emphasizes social harmony based on ordered relationships and situations. According to Confucius, peaceful life in society is ensured not by law but by morality, so the function of the law is to educate the citizenry in righteous conduct in order to maintain harmony and balance.

Japan's legal system still reflects many of these notions, though it was strongly influenced first by German and French law and later by American law. It has been described as a civil-law system with a quasi-adversarial approach to penal law (Tanaka 1976:812). Even though elaborate rules are in place for civil and criminal procedure, the Japanese have a particular aversion to litigation, and would much rather resolve disputes through conciliation. Japan is no different from any other nation in the world, in that the everyday application of the law is shaped by the attitudes and customs of ordinary people, even if it contradicts the letter of the law. Attempts were made to introduce the jury system, for example, but it never took hold. Tanaka (1976:191) notes that the disparity between "living law" and "book law" is practically universal, but the public's resistance to new ideas is especially notable when an external system has been imposed as a result of war and conquest:

> In the case of Japan, Western law based on assumptions – moral, economic, and cultural – which were widely divergent from the assumptions of the traditional life of the nation was hurriedly transplanted, primarily because of political exigencies.

As a result, new laws on domestic relations and succession, for example, do not reflect the family system of traditional Japan, and in rural areas "various devices are used to maintain the family-farming system, thus deviating in practice from what the legislators have designed" (Tanaka 1976:192). Moreover, business firms and labour unions still operate under age-old paternalistic ideals despite legislative provisions to the contrary.

International Law and Supranational Courts

In the sixteenth and seventeenth centuries, legal scholars began developing the principles of **international law**, or the **law of nations**, in order to resolve disputes that arose between two or more sovereign nations. The concepts they advanced were later incorporated into the institutions of the multinational organizations that were formed in the twentieth century, both worldwide (e.g., the United Nations, the International Labor Organization, the World Trade Organization) and regional (e.g., the European Union, the Organization of American States, the Association of South-East Asian Nations). There are now a variety of courts whose jurisdiction transcends national borders, including the International Court of Justice and the war crimes tribunals set up by the United Nations to prosecute individuals in trouble spots such as Rwanda and the Balkans, as well as the International Criminal Court that was created in Rome in 1998 for the purpose of providing a permanent venue to prosecute war crimes. Other examples are the European Court of Justice and the European Court of Human Rights in the European Union. The existence of these institutions has promoted the harmonization of national legal systems as member states strive to comply with the norms of the multinational bodies to which they belong, sometimes with fierce resistance from nationalist groups.

Conclusion

Despite the superficial similarity of the formal laws currently in place throughout the world, the practical application of those laws still varies considerably from one country to another, and from one ethnic group to another, depending on religious traditions and custom. When you work as a court interpreter, you will be mediating between two or more cultures, so it is important for you to understand not only the legal systems of the client's country of origin and his new host country, but also the prevailing attitudes toward the law in the client's community.

Suggestions for Further Reading

Adei, Christopher Y.D. (1981) *African Law South of the Sahara*, Clayton, MO: International Institute for Advanced Studies.

Derrett, J. and M. Duncan (1963) *Introduction to Modern Hindu Law,* London: Oxford University Press.

Glendon, Mary Ann, Michael Wallace Gordon and Paolo G. Carozza (1999) *Comparative Legal Traditions in a Nutshell*, St. Paul, MN: West Group.

Hassan, Farooq (1981) *The Concept of State and Law in Islam*, Washington, D.C.: University Press of America, Inc.

Leng, Shao-chuan and Hungdah Chiu (1985) *Criminal Justice in Post-Mao China: Analysis and Documents*, Albany, NY: State University of New York Press.

Merryman, John Henry and David S. Clark (1978) *Comparative Law: Western European and Latin American Legal Systems, Cases and Materials*, Indianapolis, New York, & Charlottesville, VA: The Bobbs-Merrill Company.

Moeketsi, Rosemary (1999a) *Discourse in a Multilingual and Multicultural Courtroom: A court interpreter's guide*, Pretoria: JL van Schaik.

Supreme Court of Japan (1999) *A Guide to Court Procedures* http://www.courts.go.jp/english/procedure/index.htm (30 Mar 2000).

Tanaka, Hideo (ed) (1976) *The Japanese Legal System: Introductory Cases and Materials*, Tokyo: University of Tokyo Press.

Suggestions for Further Study

1. What misunderstandings might arise between the groups you interpret for because of different legal traditions?
2. Give an example of how the daily practices of a given ethnic community conflict with the legal norms governing that community.
3. Name a feature of the legal system prevailing in your country that derives from the civil-law tradition. Name one that derives from the common-law tradition.
4. What role do you think laypersons should play in a country's legal system? State the reasons for your position.

4. Criminal and Civil Procedure

> Before an intelligent study of criminal law can be undertaken, it is
> necessary to focus on the single characteristic that differentiates it from
> civil law. This characteristic is punishment.
>
> Arnold H. Loewy (1987:1)

As a court interpreter, it is essential for you to know how cases are processed in
the courts where you work, not so that you can explain procedures to the clients
for whom you interpret, but to enable you to understand the context in which
you are operating and anticipate misunderstandings that may arise. You may be
the only interpreter involved in a given case, from police investigation and arrest through prosecution, conviction, and sentencing; or you may share the work
with various interpreters who are retained at different phases. It is particularly
important for you to understand the various stages of the proceedings if you
come into a case in the middle. In this chapter we will look at how criminal and
civil cases are processed, and then we will examine the role of the interpreter as
a function of these procedures and in light of the different legal traditions presented in the preceding chapter.

Loewy (1987:1) distinguishes between criminal law and civil law in the following manner:

> Generally, in a civil suit, the basic questions are (1) how much, if at all,
> has defendant injured plaintiff, and (2) what remedy or remedies, if any,
> are appropriate to compensate plaintiff for his loss. In a criminal case, on
> the other hand, the questions are (1) to what extent, if at all, has defend-
> ant injured society, and (2) what sentence, if any, is necessary to punish
> defendant for his transgressions.

Criminal Procedure

Most people, even the well educated, do not know how the courts operate in
their own country, simply because they do not have occasion to come into
contact with the judicial system. In fact, they may suffer from serious miscon-
ceptions if their only exposure to the law comes from television and movie
portrayals, especially if these are imported. It has been reported, for example,
that having watched countless American police dramas in which suspects are
advised of their "Miranda rights", many television viewers and movie goers in
other countries assume that they, too, have those rights. Below we will follow a
criminal case step by step, from arrest to sentencing, to explain generic criminal
procedure. You should learn the specific rules of criminal procedure in the courts
where you will be working.

Investigative Phase

A crime is usually reported to the police by the victim or the victim's family. In many countries, a distinction is made between private offences, which can be prosecuted only on the victim's initiative, and public offences, which are automatically prosecuted by the public authorities once the crime comes to their attention, regardless of the victim's wishes. In either case, the police gather initial facts and interview witnesses, and then report their findings to the public prosecutor's office. An investigation is opened, conducted either by the police under the direction of the prosecutor in common-law countries, or, in many civil-law countries, by prosecutorial authorities and the police (often a special corps known as the judicial police), under the direction of a special judge. This judge is known as an **investigative judge** or **examining magistrate** (*juge d'instruction* in France, where the concept originated).

During the investigation, witnesses are interviewed and evidence is collected and tested in the crime lab, if applicable. The prosecutor or the investigative judge must determine whether there is enough evidence to meet legal standards for continued prosecution. In the civil-law tradition, the investigative judge has an affirmative obligation to gather evidence in favour of the accused as well as evidence against him, whereas the prosecutor in a common-law system usually concerns himself only with evidence of guilt.

Once the perpetrator has been identified to the satisfaction of the prosecutor or the investigative judge, formal charges are filed and an arrest warrant is issued. In most countries, the accused has the right to remain silent, and to have defence counsel present if he consents to be questioned. He also has the right to be informed of the charges against him. After being arrested, the defendant may be released on **bail** (a pledge of money or property to guarantee appearance in court) or on **personal recognizance** (word of honour), or he may remain in custody under **preventive detention**. Usually there is a statutory limit to how long the defendant can be held before his case is heard by a judge. In many civil-law countries, the victim, or **complainant**, may be considered a civil party to the penal action, and is entitled to be represented by counsel.

In the case of serious offences, as an intermediate step, a formal showing of **probable cause** must be made to justify proceeding further with the prosecution. In common-law systems, the prosecutor must present evidence to a **grand jury**, which will decide whether to **indict** (accuse) the defendant, or, alternatively, to a magistrate in a lower court, who will decide whether to hold the defendant to answer and order him to stand trial in a higher court. In civil-law systems, the report of the investigative judge amounts to a showing of probable cause, though no equivalent term is used. In both systems, less serious offences are often dealt with in a streamlined, or **summary** proceeding, in which no intermediate step is necessary prior to the trial.

Pre-Trial Phase

Most court systems have a hierarchical structure, with specific areas of competence assigned to each court. **Courts of limited jurisdiction** (known by names
such as magistrate's court, summary court, municipal court, local court, or police court) hear minor cases and showings of probable cause in more serious
cases. Often cases are heard by a single judge in these courts. **Courts of general jurisdiction** (known as district courts, superior courts, or crown's courts)
hear more serious cases. In civil-law countries, courts of general jurisdiction
often have collegiate panels of judges who consider cases submitted to them on
the basis of the report of the investigative judge.

Offences are classified according to their seriousness; a traffic offence or a
petty theft would be considered minor, a burglary or assault would be treated as
a more serious offence, and a murder or a rape would be considered the most
serious type of crime. For example, in the United States the respective categories are **infraction**, **misdemeanor**, and **felony**; in France, they are *contravention,
délit,* and *crime.* Often the prosecutor or investigative judge has some discretion in deciding how to classify a given offence, depending on the circumstances
of the case and the defendant's background. In England these are known as
either way offences.

When the accused makes his first appearance in court, his identity is con-
firmed, defence counsel is identified, the charges are read, and often the accused
is advised of his rights as a criminal defendant. In common-law countries, at his
initial appearance the defendant must enter a **plea**, meaning an answer to the
charges; he may plead guilty, not guilty, or, in some jurisdictions, no contest or
nolo contendere (indicating that he will not dispute the prosecution's allegations, but wishes to protect himself from civil liability in case the victim sues
him in civil court). There is no plea of innocent, although that term is often
erroneously used in the press, because the defendant is presumed innocent until
proven guilty. In civil-law countries, there is no such thing as a plea, but at the
initial appearance the defendant is given an opportunity to make a statement to
the judge explaining his position.

After the formal accusation, the defence and the prosecution begin developing their cases and exchanging information in what is known as the **pre-trial
phase**. In common-law countries, during this phase the parties periodically appear in court to make motions, that is, specific requests for rulings on evidence,
discovery (revealing information to the opposing party), a postponement, ap-
pointment of experts, and so on. The other party is always given an opportunity
to respond to a motion, and the defendant is always present to hear the motions,
arguments, and rulings. During this period, the defence and prosecution may
engage in **plea bargaining**, negotiations to avoid a trial by reducing the charges
or promising lenient treatment in exchange for a guilty plea by the defendant. If

the defendant does not accept the prosecutor's offer, they proceed to trial.

In the civil-law tradition, the pre-trial process is considered the "heart" of the prosecution of crimes. In France, for example, "the crucial stage of decision-making remains (to a far greater extent than in Anglo-American juris-dictions) embedded in the bureaucratic early phases of the procedure" (Vogler 1996:17). The investigative judge gathers information by questioning witnesses and ordering the collection and testing of evidence. The judge's summaries of witness statements and the reports on the evidence are compiled in a **dossier**. This investigation is secret, and the defence and prosecution usually are not present when the judge examines witnesses. They are not allowed to see the dossier until the case is ready for trial. The investigative judge's report must be reviewed by an independent body (the *Chambre d'Accusation* in France) to ensure there is enough evidence to proceed to trial. In civil-law countries that do not have an investigative judge, such as Japan and Germany, the pre-trial phase is more open, with both sides gaining access to each other's evidence. There is no such thing as plea bargaining in legal systems that follow the civil-law tradition, although many countries have a mechanism for what is known as **consensual disposal** of cases in order to avoid the trouble and expense of a formal trial (Huber 1996).

The Trial

The trial in a criminal case is conducted very differently in civil- and common-law systems. The common-law criminal trial, perhaps carried to the ultimate extreme in the United States, is viewed by many as a "sporting match between the attorneys," while Americans counter that other countries' courts conduct trials merely as a "means of convicting the accused at any price" (Merryman and Clark 1978:705). As we will see below, both of these characterizations are exaggerations.

Under Civil Law

There is a prevalent misconception that in civil-law systems, the defendant is presumed guilty until he proves himself innocent, a false impression that prob-ably stems from the fact that the trial is very brief and usually results in conviction of the accused. In fact, the civil-law trial is simply the last step in a long process of gathering and presenting evidence, which will immediately cease if at any point it becomes apparent to the investigative judge or the prosecutor that the defendant is innocent (in that case, the charges are dismissed). There are no surprises or dramatic outbursts, because the trial amounts to a summarization of evidence already known to the parties. The investigative judge's final report is given to both defence and prosecution well before the trial so that they can prepare their cases. The real purpose of the trial is to determine the sentence to be imposed, since by this time there is no question of the defendant's guilt (Merryman and Clark 1978:701).

A typical criminal trial in a civil-law country proceeds as follows: First the charges are read, then the presiding judge informs the defendant of his rights and questions him on the facts of the case. Then the prosecution and the defence may be given an opportunity to address the court with opening statements. Following these oral arguments, any witnesses whose testimony is deemed admissible by the court are allowed to testify in a narrative form (often the testimony will focus on issues related to sentencing, such as prior criminal history and personal circumstances of the defendant). The witnesses may be examined by the presiding judge, based on questions submitted in advance by the attorneys. In some countries, witnesses may be questioned directly by counsel for the defence and prosecution; in others, all examinations are conducted by the judge. The presiding judge summarizes the testimony of each witness, and witnesses and attorneys are allowed to suggest changes if they feel the summary is not accurate. A variation on this practice can be seen in Japan, where written statements taken from witnesses may be summarized by the prosecutor if the defence consents; without the consent of the defence, witnesses must be questioned and cross-examined in person (Supreme Court of Japan 1999). Sometimes physical evidence, known as **exhibits**, is examined at trial in addition to the oral evidence presented by witnesses.

After the evidence is examined, the prosecutor, the defence attorney, and the victim's counsel (if applicable) make oral presentations. Sometimes the accused also addresses the court. In most civil-law jurisdictions, defendants are prohibited from testifying under oath, whereas witnesses usually take an oath to tell the truth before giving statements or testifying in court. These presentations generally focus on the sentence that should be imposed, with the prosecution arguing for rigorous punishment and the defence advocating leniency.

Once all arguments have been completed, the panel of judges deliberates and issues a judgement, which includes the penalty to be imposed. Sometimes this takes place immediately; in other cases, there may be a waiting period before sentence is passed. In many countries, the panel consists of a combination of professional and lay judges or **assessors**. Some civil-law countries, such as France, even have randomly selected lay juries that hear evidence and reach a verdict together with the judges (Vogler 1996). As noted above, lesser offences may be tried in summary proceedings, usually before a single judge, and sentencing takes place immediately after the cases are presented.

The judicial authority plays a very active role in determining how a civil-law trial will proceed. According to Huber (1996:110), "The fundamental duty of the court is to search for the truth and the participants have no control over the presentation of evidence nor any power to seek a discontinuance of the proceedings". The court has an obligation to establish the facts independently of the cases presented by the parties, and can even summon witnesses on its own motion. In contrast, in common-law countries the judge plays a more passive role. Hatchard (1996:184) describes the approach taken by the common law as follows:

> Central to the whole system is that the truth will emerge if equal adversaries are left to present their cases and then to test the evidence of the other party. The prosecution and the defence both separately prepare their own case, call, examine and cross-examine their witnesses.

Some countries' courts have a hybrid system. For example, Japan is considered to fall within the civil-law family, but its trial procedure is adversarial, in that "parties take the initiative in gathering and offering evidence though the court may examine evidence if necessary" (Supreme Court of Japan 1999).

Under Common Law

Many people all over the world are familiar with the way common-law criminal trials are conducted, having seen television or movie dramatizations or broadcasts of actual trials in the United States. The criminal trial is an attractive subject for writers, because it is very much like a stage play in which the story of the crime is reenacted for the audience – the jury – and attorneys employ all their persuasive powers to portray the facts in a certain light so that the jury will find in their favour. But dramatizations exaggerate certain aspects of the jury trial, and news coverage may distort the picture as well, so it is useful to review the main elements of common-law trial procedure here.

Although it is possible to have a trial without a jury, known as a **bench trial**, in which a single judge is the trier of fact and issues both the verdict and the sentence, most trials are held before a jury. The selection of the jury is the first stage of the trial. Citizens who have been summoned for jury duty assemble in the courtroom and answer questions under oath to determine whether they are qualified to serve on the jury. Anyone who might have a bias for or against the defendant, because he knows individuals involved in the case, has been the victim of a similar crime himself, or has some interest in the outcome of the case, is eliminated from the jury. Prospective jurors are warned that the trial may last several days, or even weeks or months in complex cases, and they are asked if they can make that commitment to the court. This questioning, called **voir dire**, may be conducted entirely by the judge, or partly by the judge and partly by the attorneys.

The defendant is always present during jury selection and may express opinions to the defence attorney about particular prospective jurors. Both the defence and the prosecution are allowed to exercise a limited number of **peremptory**

challenges, meaning that they can reject prospective jurors without stating the reason. It should be noted that in England and Wales, the defence is no longer allowed to make such challenges, and the prosecution rarely exercises them; whereas in the United States, these challenges are considered a very important part of the trial. After both sides are satisfied with the jury (or they have exhausted their allocation of challenges), the jury is sworn in. Most juries consist of twelve people, but in some cases in some jurisdictions, smaller juries are allowed.

The trial begins with an **opening statement** by each side to give the jury an overview of the evidence that will be presented. The adversarial nature of the proceedings becomes apparent immediately, as the attorneys make persuasive speeches intended to encourage the jury to view the case in a certain light. (These speeches may be very challenging to interpret for the defendant.) Because the prosecutor has the burden of proof, the prosecution (known as the **State**, the **People**, or the **Crown**) presents its case first and the defence then responds with its own evidence. Prosecution witnesses may include the victim, eye witnesses, police officers, criminalists and other expert witnesses, and anyone who has knowledge of some aspect of the case.

The prosecutor questions each witness in **direct examination** or **examination-in-chief** to elicit certain facts for the jury to hear. In important cases, witnesses may have undergone extensive preparation for their testimony (though the "coaching" of witnesses is forbidden), and in any case they will have told their story repeatedly by the time the case comes to trial. This may be the first time the defence has heard them, however. After all the facts have been laid out to the prosecutor's satisfaction, the defence attorney begins the **cross-examination**, questions designed to shed a critical light on the witness's testimony. After the cross-examination, the prosecutor is allowed to rehabilitate the witness in **redirect**, followed by **recross**, and so on, until the attorneys are satisfied that they have wrung every possible fact out of the witness. The process begins again with the next prosecution witness.

In addition, at any point during the testimony, one side or the other may interrupt and raise **objections** if they think the rules of evidence are violated by a question or answer, and the judge will rule on the objection. Because jurors are not trained in the law, they do not know the rules for weighing evidence, and one side will always try to take advantage of that vulnerability, while the other side will object and ask that the judge intervene to ensure proper conduct. In addition to oral evidence, physical objects, known as **exhibits**, are also presented to demonstrate facts. These items can be as varied as a letter, a cancelled check, a bloody shirt, a bullet fragment, or a photograph. Each time one side wants to introduce an exhibit into evidence, the other side has an opportunity to object, and the judge rules on its admissibility.

After the prosecution evidence has been presented, the prosecutor **rests**, and the defence has an opportunity to present its case. It is usually much shorter than the prosecution case, and in fact the defence may not call any witnesses at all. During this stage it is the defence attorney who conducts the direct examination of witnesses, and the prosecutor who cross-examines them. The defendant may or may not choose to testify, and the jury will be instructed not to consider the significance of a defendant's decision not to testify. After the defence rests, the prosecution has one more opportunity to present evidence, known as **rebuttal**, by calling new witnesses or recalling previous witnesses to reinforce its case. Then each side makes a final argument to the jury, known as a **summation** or **closing argument**, another persuasive speech to convince the jury to vote for acquittal or conviction.

After the summations, the judge instructs the jury on the law that it must apply to the facts it finds in the case, in a process known as the **jury charge** or **jury instructions**. The judge normally reads from a book of instructions especially written for the purpose of informing lay juries about certain aspects of the law. The language of these instructions tends to be very stilted and archaic, however, and they are also very challenging for interpreters. In each case, a different set of instructions is read, depending on what the attorneys and the judge agree upon. They include definitions of legal concepts such as circumstantial evidence and hearsay evidence, a listing of the elements of the offences with which the defendant is charged (known as **counts**), and guidelines for jury deliberations. After the judge has read the instructions, the jury begins secret deliberations. Eventually, the jury votes on a verdict, guilty or not guilty, for each offence charged. In most penal cases, a unanimous verdict is required. A jury that fails to reach a unanimous verdict is called a **hung jury**, and in that case the judge must declare a **mistrial**. If the verdict is "not guilty", the defendant is acquitted of all charges and is released. Any bail posted is **exonerated**, or returned. If the verdict is "guilty", the defendant is ordered to return to court for sentencing, and bail will probably be applied toward any fine that is due.

The Sentence

As noted above, in civil-law systems the penalty is part of the ruling issued by the judges at the conclusion of the trial. In the common-law system, the judge determines the penalty that will be imposed only after the jury finds the defendant guilty. Thus, the term **sentence** refers only to the penalty, not the verdict; sometimes this distinction is difficult to make in translation. Normally, before passing sentence a judge will refer the defendant to a **probation officer**, who will investigate the defendant's background and make a recommendation to the court. The probation report is given to the parties when they appear in court for sentencing, and each side is given an opportunity to address the court before the judge imposes the sentence.

Penalties in criminal cases are very similar in civil-law and common-law countries. They may include a term of incarceration, part of which may be suspended for a period of **probation** or conditional release, restrictions on the offender's activities and rights, a monetary fine, or community service. Corporal punishment has been outlawed in most of the world, and capital punishment is increasingly rare. Some states in the United States do impose the death penalty, but in those cases the judge does not issue the sentence. Instead, a special trial is held after the guilty verdict for the jury to decide on whether to impose the death penalty or life in prison. Death penalties are automatically appealed.

Appeals

In modern legal systems, whenever a litigant is dissatisfied with the ruling of a trial court (**court of original jurisdiction** or **court of the first instance**), he can appeal that ruling to a higher court (**court of appeals** or **court of the second instance**). In some cases, especially when issues of constitutionality arise, the appeals court's decision can, in turn, be appealed to the supreme court or constitutional court (**court of last resort**). Grounds for appeal vary tremendously from one country to another. In common-law systems, a verbatim record is made of the proceedings in the trial court, and the appeals court relies on the transcript of the proceedings to determine whether any error was made. Because of that, attorneys and judges are very mindful that their words are being recorded by the court stenographer, and this may contribute even more to the theatrical nature of the proceedings. The appeals court reviews only the legal aspects of the case, not the facts. If the appeals court finds that a procedural error was made by the court of original jurisdiction, it may send the case back to be retried. In criminal cases, only the defence has the right to appeal a verdict.

In civil-law systems, both the defence and the prosecution enjoy the right of appeal. The case file in an appeal is more likely to consist of judges' summaries of evidence presented rather than a verbatim transcript. The appeals court usually reviews both the law and the facts, meaning that witnesses may be summoned to testify again or new evidence may be sought. Some countries, such as Germany, make a distinction between civil and penal cases, and allow a review of both the law and the facts only in the former. The Japanese system allows the appeals court in a *koso* (first) appeal to examine witnesses only under certain exceptional circumstances, in both civil and penal cases. In France, the appeals court is known as the *Cour de Cassation*, and it is authorized only to interpret the law, not to decide cases. Thus, in contrast to the "judge-made law" of the common-law tradition, decisions of the Court of Cassation either affirm the lower court's ruling or quash it and remand the case for reconsideration, but are not binding on any other court in any other case (Glendon et al 1999).

Alternative Programmes

In many countries, efforts are made to treat certain offences (usually those involving drug abuse or sexual deviancy, and perhaps domestic violence) through rehabilitation rather than punishment. The offender may be ordered to spend a certain period of time in a treatment facility or to undergo counseling or therapy, after which charges may be dropped or amended. This process is known by a variety of terms, including **diversion** and **deferred entry of judgement**. The cases may be heard in special courts that deal exclusively with these offences. The names of these alternative programmes are often very challenging to interpret because they contain culturally-loaded terms and bureaucratic jargon ("Fresh Start", "SB38 First-Offender Program", "Drug Awareness", "Parenting Classes", etc.).

Minors who are accused of crimes are also treated differently than adults in most countries. In order to avoid the stigma of being branded a criminal at a young age due to youthful indiscretions, juveniles are prosecuted in separate courts and subject to special programmes for treatment or rehabilitation. Often, different terminology is used for proceedings in juvenile court. In the United States, for example, there is no plea, but the minor is asked to admit or deny the allegations, and the trial is known as an **adjudication**. Juveniles who commit particularly violent offences or are found to be repeat offenders may be incarcerated, but always in separate facilities from adults. Recent legal reforms in some jurisdictions provide that older juveniles who commit particularly serious offences may be tried as adults.

Civil Procedure

As noted earlier, the term **civil law** has two different meanings. In this section, we use the term to denote the litigation of private disputes, in contrast to criminal cases. Typical issues involved in civil cases include medical malpractice, torts and damages, contract enforcement, employment relationships, debt collection, divorce, adoption, probate of wills, and certain aspects of public administration (taxation, immigration, social benefits, etc.). As with juvenile matters, different terminology may be used in civil cases. For example, in the United States, rather than **complainant**, the person who files a civil complaint is called a **plaintiff** or **petitioner**, and the party being sued is called the **defendant** or **respondent**. In the case of government administrative matters, the person who initiates the action may be known as a **claimant** or **applicant**.

Most countries have a civil court structure that is parallel to the criminal court hierarchy. In some systems, civil and penal cases arising out of the same incident (such as a car accident) may be processed together by the same court.

As with penal cases, lesser matters are heard in courts of limited jurisdiction in summary proceedings, and more serious matters (involving large amounts of money or drastic consequences for the defendant, such as loss of property) are heard in courts of general jurisdiction in more complicated and prolonged proceedings. It should be noted that no matter how serious the case, loss of liberty is never at stake; in other words, no defendant can be imprisoned as a result of a civil judgement against him.

The procedure followed in civil cases is very similar to that of criminal cases: First a complaint is filed with the court, and the defendant is notified, usually by having papers delivered or **served** in person, and is given a certain period to respond. The initial complaint and the response are known as the **pleadings**. The form of the pleadings must comply with strict rules regarding the statement of the demand for relief and the legal grounds on which the suit is based.

Next comes the evidence-gathering stage. In many civil-law countries, a judge or panel of judges receives evidence from the parties over a period of time, and may question witnesses personally or simply read their statements before issuing a ruling. In a hybrid system like Japan's, this process may occur at a single oral proceeding conducted by a judge, with direct and cross-examination of witnesses. In common-law countries, the attorneys for the parties gather evidence by submitting written questions to the parties (**interrogatories**) or taking sworn testimony outside the presence of the judge from either parties or witnesses (**depositions**) in a process called **discovery**. During this phase they try to settle the case without going to trial, and they may decide to submit the case to **binding arbitration** (in which they agree in advance to abide by the decision of a professional arbiter, often a retired judge). If they do go to trial, they can choose between a jury and a bench trial, and the procedure followed is the same as in a penal case. Japan has a similar method of avoiding trial, known as **conciliation**, with the unique feature of a Conciliation Committee composed of a professional judge and two or more lay commissioners (Supreme Court of Japan 1999).

There is no jury in civil proceedings in countries in the civil-law family, even those that do make use of the lay jury or lay judges in criminal proceedings. Consequently, there is no need to bring all the parties together at once for a formal trial; rather, civil litigation in these countries has been described as a "continuous process of meetings, hearings, and written communications during which evidence is introduced, testimony is taken, and motions are made and decided. A primary goal of the system is to facilitate settlements" (Glendon et al 1999:96). Since legal professionals rather than laypersons decide civil cases, they are given more latitude in their decision-making and do not have to observe strict rules of evidence. As in penal cases, the judge in civil proceedings plays a more active role in investigating the facts than in common-law countries. The judge may obtain certain types of evidence, such as expert opinions, on his own motion, thus "reducing the disadvangate of the party with the less competent lawyer" (Glendon et al 1999:96). The attorneys, in contrast, are just as adversarial in civil-law countries as their common-law counterparts, in that each side attempts to persuade a neutral party, the judge, that they are in the right.

The Interpreter's Role

The nature of your work as an interpreter will depend a great deal on how evidence is gathered and presented in your country's legal system. In courts where much of the evidence is submitted in writing and testimony is summarized rather than recorded verbatim, you will most likely be asked to provide a consecutive summary interpretation (modes of interpreting will be discussed further in Chapter 6). You may or may not be expected to translate documentary evidence for the defendant, depending on the laws of your country. Summarizing complex legal proceedings is a very difficult task fraught with potential for distortion, so it is all the more essential that you be familiar with the workings of the court system. Ideally, all summarizing should be done by judges or attorneys, with a complete interpretation of the summary to ensure that the defendant is fully apprised of what is happening in the case. Many courts will allow simultaneous interpretation at the request of one of the parties.

If you work in a court where a verbatim record is made and witnesses testify in person, you may be expected to provide a simultaneous interpretation of the entire proceedings for the defendant. Witness testimony presented in a foreign language is generally interpreted in the consecutive mode for the record, in as close to a verbatim manner as the target language allows; summary interpreting should be avoided. In adversarial proceedings, the trial is a dramatic event that puts a lot of pressure on all of the "performers", including the interpreter. Interpreting on the witness stand is particularly stressful, because to convey the testimony accurately so that it will have the same impact on the jury as non-interpreted testimony, you must take on the witness's demeanor as if you were acting a part in a play. Each side wants the witness's words to be interpreted in a way that favours their case, and they may object to the interpretation even when it is correct. It is very difficult to maintain the necessary impartiality when you are being pulled in both directions by the attorneys. Furthermore, the melodramatic speeches given by counsel, the arcane legal jargon of motions and objections, the rapid-fire exchanges in cross-examination, and the technical testimony of expert witnesses all pose tremendous challenges for interpretation.

It is also hard to maintain neutrality as an interpreter when cultural misunderstandings arise. It may be tempting to provide information about a certain practice, concept, or expression when you are familiar with the subject and you want to help people communicate. There is a danger, though, that you may be perceived as favouring one side or the other by speaking for them or explaining their attitudes, and in any case, you would be acting as a witness rather than an interpreter. If the court needs information about a certain culture or ethnic group, it might be better served by obtaining that information from someone who is not otherwise involved in the case, such as a college professor or a community leader. Guidelines for providing explanations or clarifications when interpreting are presented in the next chapter.

Suggestions for Further Reading

Colin, Joan and Ruth Morris (1996) *Interpreters and the Legal Process*, Winchester: Waterside Press.
Hatchard, John, Barbara Huber and Richard Vogler (eds) (1996) *Comparative Criminal Procedure*, London: British Institute of International and Comparative Law.
Loewy, Arnold H. (1987) *Criminal Law in a Nutshell*, St. Paul, MN: West Publishing Co.

Suggestions for Further Study

1. What are the rules of criminal and civil procedure in your country? How do they compare with those of the country or countries where your language is spoken?
2. What are some legal terms that are particularly difficult to interpret in your working languages?
3. If possible, observe a court proceeding and keep a journal of your experience.
4. Invite a judge or lawyer to speak to your class about a specific area of the law.
5. Take a field trip to a crime lab, a juvenile detention facility, or a police station.
6. How are juvenile matters handled in your country? How does the terminology differ from that of the adult courts?
7. Here are two figures showing the positions of the participants in a South African courtroom (Figure 1) and a Japanese courtroom (Figure 2). How does this layout compare with that of a courtroom in your country?

Figure 1: South African Courtroom

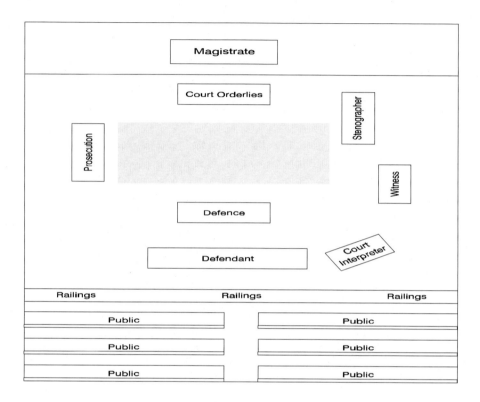

Figure 2: Japanese Courtroom

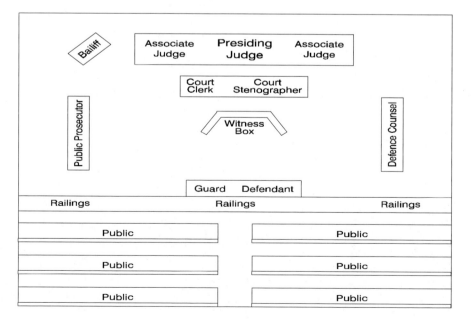

5.   The Code of Ethics

> A code of ethics does not propose a foundation for morality; nor does it offer a comprehensive theory of social justice. Ethics is the moral philosophy of practice, of decisions faced in quotidian and – especially – professional life.
>
> Jacob T. Levy (1999:72)

> A code of ethics protects the interpreter and lessens the arbitrariness of his or her decisions by providing guidelines and standards to follow.
>
> Sharon Neumann Solow (1981:39)

Every profession has a code of ethics to guide its practitioners, and interpreting is no exception. Regardless of what type of setting they work in, professional interpreters must uphold certain standards of practice, including accurate and faithful interpretation, confidentiality, and impartiality. In the legal environment, given the high stakes involved (personal liberty and property, public security) and the potential for misunderstandings and miscarriages of justice, ethical standards are especially important. Indeed, the Code of Ethics of the Austrian Association of Court Interpreters begins with a preamble that notes the court interpreter's critical role in upholding basic human rights and equality before the law. In this chapter, we will review the tenets of the ethical codes that govern court interpreters in various jurisdictions. The specific codes referred to are listed at the end of the chapter. In addition, the Code of Conduct for Court Interpreters developed by the Committee for Legal Translators and Court Interpreters of the International Federation of Translators (FIT) appears in Appendix B. Because each case is unique, and court interpreters are constantly called upon to make instantaneous decisions about appropriate behaviour, we will also present some practical guidelines for applying ethical principles in real-life situations.

Canons of the Code of Ethics

Professional associations of court interpreters usually adopt standards of practice that their members agree to uphold. In addition, many jurisdictions have regulations, statutes, or rules of court that set forth the ethical obligations of interpreters. Although specific practices vary from one court to another, there are certain universal features that characterize all codes of ethics. Those features are identified and discussed below:

1. Fidelity

The interpreter has a moral and professional – not to mention legal – obligation to convey the complete meaning of the speaker's message. A typical expression of this requirement can be found in the code of ethics promulgated by the Australian Institute of Interpreters and Translators (AUSIT):

> 5. Accuracy
> a) Truth and Completeness
>   i) In order to ensure the same access to all that is said by all parties involved in a meeting, interpreters shall relay accurately and completely everything that is said.
>   ii) Interpreters shall convey the whole message, including derogatory or vulgar remarks, as well as non-verbal clues.
>   iii) If patent untruths are uttered or written, interpreters and translators shall convey these accurately as presented.
>   iv) Interpreters and translators shall not alter, make additions to, or omit anything from their assigned work.

This code comes from a common-law country where verbatim records are made of court proceedings, but even where witness statements are summarized by the judge, it is important for the judge to hear a complete interpretation in the first person (not "He says that he saw" but "I saw") to gain an accurate perception of the speaker's intent so that it can be reflected in the summary. In other words, any editing that takes place should be done by the judge, not the interpreter. The same holds true for interpreting in police interrogations or interviews by attorneys.

It is particularly important to refrain from simplifying complex or technical language for the "benefit" of an unsophisticated defendant or witness. Although your natural inclination may be to make sure the listener fully understands the message, in the courtroom setting such well-intentioned editing distorts the legal process, particularly in an adversarial system. The *Model Code of Professional Responsibility for Interpreters in the Judiciary*, published by the National Center for State Courts in the United States, asserts in its preamble that linguistic barriers to communication faced by non-English-speaking litigants should be removed "as far as possible, so that these persons are placed in the same position as similarly situated persons for whom there is no such barrier", and it further clarifies in a footnote, "A non-English speaker should be able to understand just as much as an English speaker with the same level of education and intelligence". This cautionary note is intended to underline the fact that many laypersons who appear in court are baffled by the language and behaviour of court personnel, and the litigant who happens to need an interpreter should not be at an advantage compared to one who speaks the language of the court.

The question of what constitutes an accurate interpretation is, of course, a complex one. Translation theorists have been debating the issue for centuries, and this is not the place to further that discussion. Suffice it to say that meaning is contained in both linguistic elements (e.g., words, phrases, grammatical structures) and non-linguistic elements (e.g., tone of voice, pauses, facial expressions, gestures) of a message, and you must account for all elements of meaning in your renditions in the target language. The reproduction of witness gestures is a complex issue. It can be argued that everyone in the courtroom can see the witness and there is no need for the court interpreter to repeat any movements or facial expressions made by the witness. Certain gestures are culture-specific, however, and might be misunderstood without some explanation. As a court interpreter, you must therefore exercise a great deal of discretion in deciding whether intervention is required to convey the full meaning of the witness's testimony.

The interpreter is also obliged to inform the parties of any impediment to a faithful interpretation, such as the inability to hear or understand a speaker, excessively lengthy statements that overtax the memory, rapid speech, or fatigue from long spells of interpreting without a break. If at any point you become aware of an error in your interpretation, you must inform the parties immediately (this may happen even after you have completed an interpreting assignment). Whereas in other settings it may be acceptable for interpreters to gloss over minor gaps in understanding or to generalize when they do not know a specific term, in legal interpreting you must always state clearly when you do not understand something or cannot recall a detail.

If you are interpreting in a situation where a verbatim record is being made, you should always clearly distinguish between statements you are interpreting and statements you are making yourself in your capacity as interpreter. In the United States, the standard practice is for interpreters to refer to themselves in the third person ("By the interpreter: Could the question be repeated please?" or "The interpreter would like to make a correction").

2. *Confidentiality*

The first item under Section 4. Ethical and Professional Issues in the *National Register of Public Service Interpreters' Code of Conduct* (United Kingdom) states that interpreters shall "respect confidentiality at all times and not seek to take advantage of any information disclosed during their work". In Spain, not only must court interpreters refrain from revealing information about the cases they interpret, they must also keep secret the identity of the parties for whom they interpret, unless they are expressly authorized to divulge that information (Márquez Villegas 1997).

It is a recognized principle of law that anything discussed between an attorney and client is "privileged", meaning that neither party can be forced to reveal what they said. An interpreter who mediates that conversation falls under the attorney-client privilege. There are certain exceptions to this rule, however. The *Code of Practice* of the Australian Institute of Interpreters and Translators (AUSIT) notes in Section 2.a.ii. that "Disclosure of information may be permissible with clients' agreement or when disclosure is mandated by law". If there is imminent danger, for example, or if a crime is about to be committed, in many countries the privilege becomes invalid. Another situation in which information about a case may be revealed by an interpreter is when other interpreters coming in to work on the case need to be briefed. "In such circumstances, the ethical obligation for confidentiality extends to all members of the team and/or agency", according to the AUSIT guidelines (Section 2.a.iii.).

Interpreters are generally cautioned not to make any public comment about cases they are assigned to interpret. Sometimes trials become the subject of public controversy, and news reporters may approach the interpreter for "inside information". It is important to resist the temptation to express opinions or even talk about how the trial is going in general terms, because such statements could be construed as showing bias on the interpreter's part and could become grounds for appeal. On the other hand, interpreters do need to consult with colleagues and other experts about technical terms or ethical dilemmas that arise in their work. It is perfectly acceptable for you to discuss aspects of a case as part of your research and professional development, as long as you do not reveal names or other sensitive information that might compromise confidentiality.

3. *Impartiality*

Interpreters in all settings are expected to remain impartial, whether they are working at a conference, a seminar, a business meeting, or a press conference. This is especially true in litigation, since the parties are by definition in conflict with each other, and they want to make sure the interpreter does not distort language in a way that favours the other side. According to Article 4 of the *Code of Conduct for Court Interpreters* of the International Federation of Translators (FIT), "The court interpreter shall at all times be neutral and impartial and shall not allow his/her personal attitudes or opinions to impinge upon the performance of his/her duties".

Gile (1995:29) prefers the term "rotating side-taking" to describe the interpreter's obligation to his clients: If "the interpreter works alternately for opposing speakers, his or her *loyalty* shifts from one to the other as he or she interprets them" (emphasis in original). He notes that this may be difficult to achieve in highly emotional situations, but professional interpreters are accustomed to keeping their personal reactions in check. He goes on to say that "as long as the interpreter speaks *in the first person* ... there is an ethical obligation to adopt the Sender-loyalty principle" (Gile 1995:31, emphasis in original), the "sender" being the source-language speaker. The corollary is that interpreting in the third person relieves the interpreter of this "Sender loyalty", but third-person interpreting is not considered appropriate for the court setting.

Although the parties' differing interests may be more apparent in an adversarial legal system, the neutrality of the interpreter is always essential in any legal setting. Consequently, if the interpreter has close ties with one of the parties (kinship or a business relationship, for example), or has a personal or financial interest in the outcome of the case, there is a conflict of interest and the interpreter should be disqualified. The code of ethics governing court interpreters in Austria, for example, states in Article 3, "The interpreter shall not use information acquired during the course of his employment for his own ends". Several codes further caution interpreters against referring clients to law firms or other businesses even if they do not have a financial interest in the business, because of the appearance of bias that would be created.

Merely being acquainted with a party does not create a conflict of interest, but in some situations it is obviously impossible to remain impartial, as when the interpreter is a close relative of the defendant. Other conflicts of interest are more subtle. Suppose an interpreter in a rape case has been a rape victim herself. It is highly unlikely that she would be able to interpret testimony in an unbiased manner. Another example is an interpreter who is also a police officer. Even if the individual has not acted in a law-enforcement capacity in the case at hand, i.e., did not arrest the suspect and has not participated in the investigation of the facts, there is still an inherent bias in the interpreter's approach to the case. If you have any doubts about whether you have a conflict of interest, it is best to confer with a judge or other neutral authority who can assess the situation properly. It is also a good idea to disclose to all parties any relationship that might create a potential or apparent conflict of interest, while assuring them of your ability to remain objective.

Another aspect of impartiality that interpreters need to consider is the acceptance of payment. By definition, professional interpreters are paid for their services, but this does not mean that they owe loyalty to the person paying them. Interpreters serve justice and the judicial system in general, and they owe their loyalty to the interpreting profession. Whether you are paid by the court, a law enforcement agency, the law office that has requested your services, or the individual litigant for whom you are interpreting, you have an obligation to interpret accurately to the best of your ability, regardless of the impact that may have on the parties' cases. Under no circumstances should you ever accept payment in addition to the fee you normally charge for services or agree to any fee contingent on the outcome of the case. A grateful litigant may wish to reward you after winning his case, but such gratuities should be politely declined. Accepting additional payment might give the impression that your performance could be altered with inducements. The code of conduct published by the Registry of Interpreters for the Deaf (United States) sums up this principle in its Tenet 5: "Interpreters/transliterators shall request compensation for services in a professional and judicious manner".

There is a natural tendency for people who do not speak the official language of the courts to view the interpreter as an ally, a lifeline, especially if they are in a desperate situation. They may ask the interpreter for advice about what they should do or what is going to happen to them. It is tempting to answer such questions by reassuring the person or explaining how the system works. You may sympathize with him, or you may be disdainful of him because he broke the law. Remember, though, that your real client is the court and the justice system, not an individual for whom you may be interpreting at the moment, and you must keep your own emotions in check and remain impartial. This neutral attitude is often described as "professional detachment" (Colin and Morris 1996).

Sometimes there is an appearance of partiality, when in fact the interpreter is quite objective. Unfortunately, just belonging to the same ethnic group as the defendant may give some people the impression that the interpreter is "on his side". While there is nothing you can do about other people's prejudices, you can prevent the appearance of bias by avoiding extraneous conversations with any of the parties. Above all, you should not have any independent conversation with a person for whom you are interpreting, because it will look like you are giving them advice or interfering with their testimony. You should also refrain from expressing any personal opinions or emotional reactions to what you are interpreting. It is important that everyone in the courtroom views you as unbiased so that they will trust in the accuracy of your interpretation.

Parties who must rely on an interpreter are forced to relinquish control over the communication, and they are naturally distrustful. Until they are assured that everything is being interpreted accurately, they will worry that the interpreter may betray them or distort what is being said. How can you reassure your clients if they don't understand what you are saying? In addition to refraining from extraneous conversations, as noted above, you can gain the confidence of all parties by observing professional conduct.

4. Professional Conduct

Canon 4 of the *Model Code of Professional Responsibility for Interpreters in the Judiciary*, which governs court interpreters in much of the United States, provides that "Interpreters shall conduct themselves in a manner consistent with the dignity of the court and shall be as unobtrusive as possible". In other words, you should not call undue attention to yourself when interpreting testimony, so that everyone in the courtroom can focus on the witness; and you should not disrupt the proceedings by interpreting too loudly or obstructing sight lines. You should be sure to observe the protocol of the court where you are working, which includes using the proper forms of address for courtroom personnel ("Your Honour", "My Lord", "Counsel", etc.), and bowing or standing and sitting at the appropriate times. Several of the codes cited here also mention punctuality and courtesy. The AUSIT code, for instance, requires that interpreters be "polite and courteous at all times" as well as "unobtrusive, but firm and dignified" (Sections 1.a.i. and 1.a.iii.).

Professional conduct also refers to relations with colleagues. The Spanish code of ethics for judiciary interpreters, for example, requires that interpreters help their colleagues, present and future, and refrain from expressing opinions about the competence of other interpreters (Sections 2.2.7 and 2.2.8). The Austrian code states in Article 6, "The court interpreter shall always aim to cooperate effectively with his colleagues". The AUSIT code has a section called "Infamous Conduct", in which it declares, "Interpreters and translators shall refrain from behaviour which their colleagues would reasonably regard as unprofessional or dishonourable" (Section 1.d.). The latter code and the one developed by the National Register of Public Service Interpreters in the United Kingdom also contain extensive provisions for resolving disputes or complaints, either by interpreters or by clients. Solidarity with colleagues is essential for maintaining the dignity of the profession and earning the respect of other legal professionals.

Another important aspect of professional conduct is honesty and integrity. Most of the codes of ethics contain provisions asserting that interpreters should not accept assignments for which they are not qualified (e.g., Article 5 of the Austrian code), and that once they accept an assignment, they should prepare adequately by gathering as much information as possible about the nature of the case and conducting any necessary research (e.g., Section 1.c. of the AUSIT code). If at any point they become aware of a problem in rendering competent interpreting services, they must notify the client. In the words of the U.S. Model Code, Canon 8, "Interpreters shall assess at all times their ability to deliver their services. When interpreters have any reservation about their ability to satisfy an assignment competently, they shall immediately convey that reservation to the appropriate judicial authority". For example, if you are asked to interpret for a witness and you discover upon arrival at the court that she speaks a dialect you are not familiar with, you should withdraw from the case. Similarly, if the testimony turns to a technical subject matter you did not anticipate and you do not know the correct terminology, you should inform the court and request a recess to research the terms, or request that an interpreter more conversant with the subject matter at hand be assigned to the case.

Professional development is another key element of professionalism for court interpreters. A typical requirement in this regard is Tenet 7 of the code promulgated by the Registry of Interpreters for the Deaf in the United States: "Interpreters/transliterators shall strive to further their knowledge and skills through participation in workshops, professional meetings, interaction with professional colleagues, and reading of current literature in the field". As González et al (1991:518-519) note,

> Because human language is dynamic and ever changing, it is extremely important for court interpreters to keep abreast of the latest changes in usage, both by the public at large and by the specialized groups for whom they interpret (the legal community, court personnel, immigrant communities, gangs, and so on). Moreover, interpreting skills themselves require constant honing. For this reason, continuing education is a vital part of the interpreters' professional activities.

Practical Guidelines

In an article on ethics, Jacob T. Levy (1999:72-73) states,

> One of the things people do in their day-to-day lives is make morally important decisions, and often it's hard to identify the right choice. It's difficult even in those professions, such as law, that have specialized and explicitly codified rules of ethics. And for people who aren't in such professions, guidance is hard to come by.

Court interpreters do have codes of ethics to guide them, but learning and internalizing basic ethical principles such as confidentiality and impartiality may not be enough to help them make the split-second, high-stakes decisions that come up so frequently in court. Moreover, the other players in the courtroom (including, unfortunately, judges and lawyers) are not familiar with the interpreter's code of ethics, and may inadvertently ask the interpreter to violate it. As Hale and Luzardo (1997:10) point out,

> Even though a number of complementary codes of ethics exist ..., these are unknown to the interpreters' "clients". We often find therefore, that either the service provider or, more likely, the non English speaker, will expect the interpreter to act in a way contrary to what is recommended by the Code of Ethics. This may be due to plain ignorance of the role of the interpreter or to the fact that for a number of reasons, non English speakers have at one stage or another been aided by a friend, child or other relative, or a non professional interpreter, who has not adhered to the Code of Ethics, resulting in confusion for the client about what is to be expected from the interpreter.

For example, any court interpreter who has gone through even the most rudi-
mentary training programme can regurgitate the tenet "Interpreters shall not
give legal advice"; but sometimes a request for legal advice is not so easy to
recognize. Suppose that during a break in the proceedings the defendant says to
the interpreter, "They're accusing me of 'conspiracy'. What does that mean?"
A well-meaning interpreter might try to be helpful by answering that question,
but in fact it requires legal expertise to answer accurately, and the interpreter
will find him/herself on a slippery slope leading to practising law without a
licence. Even if he/she recognizes that it is unethical to answer the question,
he/she is hard-pressed to find a way to decline without appearing to be rude or
ignorant. Alternatively, if a judge tells an interpreter not to interpret a statement he/she makes on the bench in open court, the interpreter may be aware
that he/she has an obligation to interpret everything, but is too intimidated by
the judge to speak up.

Because similar dilemmas arise constantly in the interpreter's day-to-day
work, and because a code of ethics is not designed to provide an answer for
every specific problem, it is helpful to learn how to respond to real-life situations in a safe environment by engaging in role-playing exercises. Rehearsing
effective responses will make it easier to say the right thing under pressure in
the courtroom. Below are some practical guidelines, presented in the form of
answers to typical questions from novice interpreters, followed by some scenarios for role-playing to help you develop your own responses to ethical
dilemmas.

What should I do when I go to court for the first time?

First impressions are extremely important. It is a good idea to go to the court
where you will be working the day before your interpreting assignment to learn
the layout of the courthouse and observe the behaviour and dress of court personnel. On the day of your assignment, wear appropriate attire and arrive early
at the courthouse. Report to the clerk's office (or whatever office is responsible
for hiring interpreters), introduce yourself, and find out what courtroom(s) you
will be working in. This is also an appropriate time to discuss payment and
billing procedures. As soon as you arrive in the courtroom, introduce yourself
to the relevant court personnel and identify the parties who will require your
services. Then introduce yourself to the parties and explain your role, as indi-
cated below. When you have completed your interpreting assignment, before
leaving check with the clerk to make sure you are not needed for another witness or in another courtroom. Such common courtesies are important for
maintaining professional relationships and will ensure that you are called again
to interpret in that court.

How can I prepare myself for interpreting assignments?

When you are given an interpreting assignment, find out what kind of case(s) you will be interpreting for (criminal or civil, nature of the charges or complaints, whether you will be interpreting for witnesses or the defendant) and how long the proceeding is likely to last. Request permission to view the case file before the proceedings start so that you can familiarize yourself with the facts and begin researching terms. (Court personnel may be reluctant to provide you with this information, especially if they are not accustomed to working with professional interpreters. If you explain to them that this is a normal part of preparation for an interpreting assignment that will enable you to do an adequate job, they are more likely to cooperate.) Ask for the names of the attorneys involved so that you can contact them and find out more about the nature of the case. When you determine what the case is about, begin assembling the appropriate dictionaries, glossaries, and other references.

Is it all right if I bring dictionaries to court? Won't people doubt my competence if they see me looking up terms?

Dictionaries and glossaries are indispensable working tools for the interpreter. Lawyers and judges frequently consult legal references during the course of their work, and interpreters are no different. Of course, you should be proficient enough in your working languages that you do not have to look up terms that one could normally expect to encounter in a court proceeding; but there is always the possibility that an unfamiliar term will arise, and you should be prepared to deal with it. If you exhibit the professional demeanor discussed previously in this chapter, your clients will have confidence in your abilities.

What should I say when I introduce myself?

When you introduce yourself to court personnel, state your name and hand them a business card, if you have one, and tell them the language you interpret and the case you have been assigned to. In the case of the lawyers, you should also ascertain whether they have worked with interpreters before and are familiar with your role. If you feel it is appropriate, remind them that you will interpret everything that is said in court, and that you are not allowed to give legal advice or perform any tasks beyond interpreting, such as explaining documents or procedures. Explain that you would like to meet with the witness or client and briefly explain your role. When you introduce yourself to the defendant or witness you will be interpreting for, you may also want to say something like this:

> Have you ever worked with an interpreter before? Please bear in mind that I will interpret everything you say, and everything everyone else says in the courtroom, as if they were my own words. Please don't say

anything you do not want to have interpreted. I'm not allowed to explain or clarify anything, so if you have any questions, please direct them to the judge or to your lawyer, and I will interpret for you. When you are testifying, if you are going to give a long answer, please pause frequently to allow me to interpret phrase by phrase so that I can interpret as accurately as possible. Do you have any trouble understanding me? Do you have any questions?

Note that in this brief interview with the client, there is no discussion of the facts in the case, so there is no danger of your being prejudiced or influencing the testimony in any way. When the person answers your questions, you will have an opportunity to become accustomed to his or her accent, speaking style, and vocabulary. If your reading of the case file has led you to believe there may be problems with the translation of a critical term, you may ask the client what term he or she uses for that concept or object.

Some jurisdictions have developed standard instructions to be read by the judge to the different parties in an interpreted case so that they will understand the role of the interpreter. An example of such instructions can be found in Appendix A.

What if a witness or lawyer uses a term I don't know?

Under no circumstances should you guess at an unknown term or omit it from your interpretation. Inform the court that you are unable to interpret it and ask permission either to consult your dictionary or to request clarification from the person who used the term. Make sure you avoid having any conversation with any of the parties without first informing the court of the situation, so as not to raise suspicions among those who do not understand the language you are speaking. For example, you might say, "Your Honour, the witness has used a term the interpreter is not familiar with. May the interpreter inquire?" It is advisable to refer to yourself in the third person to make it clear to everyone that you are not interpreting the witness's words, but are speaking as the interpreter.

A related problem is vague or ambiguous statements, which are sometimes difficult to interpret with the same degree of ambiguity in the target language. The pronoun "you" in English can be either singular or plural, for example, and you may need to clarify what is meant before you can interpret it accurately. On the other hand, some questions and answers may be deliberately vague, and attempts by the interpreter to clarify them could interfere with the examination of the witness (this is particularly true in adversarial proceedings). Therefore, you should be very cautious about intervening to request clarification.

What if I realize I made a mistake in my interpretation of earlier testimony?

Inform the court of the error and correct the mistake as soon as you become aware of it. You might say something like, "The interpreter would like to correct the record. Previously when I said 'red' I should have said 'purple'". It is never too late to correct an error; even if you have completed your assignment and gone home, you should still go back to the court and report the error.

What if the speaker makes an obvious mistake?
Simply interpret the erroneous statement. Even if it is a slip of the tongue, such as addressing the witness by the wrong name or misquoting a date, it should be interpreted as is. Always remember that if there were no interpreter present, the error would still be made and it would go uncorrected.

What if I forget part of a statement that I'm interpreting consecutively?
Inform the court that you need to have the statement repeated. You should develop your memory and note taking skills to the point that requests for repetitions are rare occurrences, but all interpreters need them now and then. If you use the proper protocol and don't ask for repetitions too frequently, no one will doubt your competence as an interpreter.

What if the parties address me directly instead of each other?
Often lawyers who are not accustomed to working with interpreters will preface a question with "Ask him if he saw..." rather than "Did you see ..." A gentle reminder is usually sufficient to break this habit. You might ask the court, "Could counsel be instructed to address the witness directly rather than in the third person?" If this practice persists, simply interpret the question as it is asked. The witness may very well respond with "Whom do you want me to ask?", which will serve as another reminder. If the witness addresses you directly ("Tell him that ..."), follow the same procedure. Sometimes a witness will refer to the interpreter in testimony, saying something like "Well, he was about as far away as you are from me". In that case, you may inform the court that the witness was referring to you, the interpreter.

What if one of the parties uses inappropriate language or says something I know will not be understood correctly?
Courtroom testimony, especially in criminal cases, sometimes involves obscene language or graphic descriptions of sex or violence. Although it may embarrass you to interpret such language, you have an obligation to interpret faithfully, without omitting or altering the tone. It may help you to bear in mind that judges and lawyers have heard this kind of testimony many times before, and they know you are performing your duty by interpreting these words. Remember that the witness's credibility is being judged and the facts determined on the basis of this testimony, and it should not be distorted for the sake of decorum.

Another common problem is that the highly sophisticated language used by judges and lawyers may not be understood by laypersons with little or no formal education. It may be tempting to simplify a question posed in very formal language, such as, "Prior to the incident in question, had you ever visited the residence of the decedent?" when you know that the witness is not likely to understand it. Suppose you rendered the question as "Before the killing, had you been to the victim's house?" If the witness gave a straightforward answer, everyone in the courtroom would assume he understood the original question, and they would misperceive his level of sophistication. If you interpreted the question at the high register of the original, the witness would probably respond with a blank look, a non-responsive answer, or a request for clarification, and the problem would become apparent to all. Then the lawyer could rephrase the question however he saw fit, and you would not be taking the responsibility of making the question understandable.

Yet another typical problem is references to cultural notions that do not exist in the target language. Kinship terms, for example, vary tremendously from one language to another. Sometimes determining the exact relationship between two people is critical, and an explanation may be required. On the other hand, sometimes the term is just a passing reference to someone and can be rendered more generically (e.g., "He is my cousin," rather than "He is the youngest son of my mother's eldest brother"). If an explanation is required, it is best to simply inform the court that there is a cultural issue, without offering the explanation yourself, and suggest that the witness be asked to clarify in his own words. As the court interpreter, you are a language expert, and you are not necessarily qualified to give testimony about cultural practices. An example of a cultural difference that requires a more comprehensive solution is the concept of guilt. González et al (1991:533) and Moeketsi (1999b:15) point out that some cultures have no such concept, so this essential element of criminal law cannot be translated. If you are aware of such a problem in your language combination, you can alert the judge and attorneys to it ahead of time so that they can plan extra time for explanations and possibly even call in expert witnesses.

What if I realize in the middle of an interpreting assignment that I am not able to do an adequate job?

If the problem is that the proceedings become complicated and technical and you are not prepared to deal with the terminology, you may ask for a recess to obtain the appropriate resources and conduct research, or you may recommend a colleague who is more qualified to handle the case. You may discover that a witness or defendant speaks a dialect that you have trouble understanding, in which case you should immediately inform the court so that another interpreter can be found. If you find that you are overwhelmed by the pace of the proceedings or the emotional atmosphere, you may request a break. In short, whenever any problem arises that interferes with your ability to interpret properly, such as rapid speech, inaudibility, technical complexity, or fatigue, you should inform the court so that appropriate steps can be taken. To prevent fatigue and the resultant errors, lengthy proceedings should be interpreted by pairs of interpreters who spell each other at intervals of 30 to 45 minutes, following the practice of conference interpreters.

Should I mimic the witness's testimony exactly, with the same tone of voice, facial expressions, and gestures?

All of these elements are part of the message and should be accounted for in the interpretation. If the witness is uncertain and speaks hesitantly, your interpretation should reflect all of the hedges, self-corrections, and fragmented ideas of the original. On the other hand, there is a fine line between interpreting precisely and making a mockery of the proceedings. If you were to burst into tears or pound on the table exactly as the witness did, you would turn the testimony into a comedy routine, and the people in the courtroom would end up paying more attention to the spectacle than to the content of the witness's testimony. Therefore, you should retain the emphasis of the original while slightly attenuating your tone of voice. Actions such as crying and grimacing can be seen by everyone in the courtroom and do not need to be reproduced unless there is a potential for misunderstanding due to cultural differences. If the witness points to a place in the courtroom or a part of his body, or indicates a measurement or motion with her hands, you should just interpret the words accompanying the gesture ("He hit me here", "It was about this long", etc.). In proceedings where a verbatim record is being made, the judge or the examining counsel can describe the witness's actions for the record.

Note that while it is appropriate to reflect the emotions of the witness in your interpretation, it is not appropriate to display your own emotions. Sometimes testimony in court cases can be rather shocking, and exhibits such as graphic photographs of the crime scene or bloody clothing may be introduced into evidence. On other occasions, parties may make humorous remarks, wittingly or unwittingly. In all these cases it is important for you to suppress your own reactions and remain impartial and detached.

How do I respond when a judge or lawyer tells me to do something I know is unethical?

Fending off requests to violate the code of ethics is a delicate task, especially when dealing with someone with the authority of a judge. Suppose a judge tells you to make sure the accused understands his/her rights. You could say, "Your Honour, my code of ethics prohibits me from explaining things, as that would amount to giving legal advice, but I will gladly interpret anything you or his counsel wishes to explain to him". This is a polite and respectful way of declining to perform the task while suggesting an alternative. On the other hand, you may be asked by defence attorneys, prosecutors, investigators, or police officers to perform tasks that are unethical, such as revealing information you have acquired during the course of your interpreting, or taking a statement or otherwise obtaining information from the client or witness. These may be people with whom you work on a daily basis, and you want to maintain good relations with them. In this case, though you will still decline to perform the task, you may want to use an informal and humorous tone: "Oh, come on, you know I can't do that. Let's agree that I stick to interpreting and you stick to practising law (or enforcing the law, as the case may be)".

As Hale and Luzardo (1997) have remarked, the laypersons for whom we interpret often misunderstand our role as well. For example, it is common for defendants to ask their interpreter, whom they regard as an ally, what they should do, how the trial is going, or whether their lawyer is any good. Although interpreters know they should not answer such questions, it is hard to decline without appearing to be discourteous, and they do want to maintain a relationship of trust with the client. It is best to avoid being in a situation that encourages such questions in the first place. In other words, you should not sit with the accused while waiting for the case to be called or during a break in the proceedings. Distancing yourself from the defendant in this way not only saves you from dealing with inappropriate questions, but also helps you avoid the appearance of bias created by conversing with the defendant, and gives you a much-needed rest from talking. If somehow you do find yourself being asked questions by a defendant or witness, you can politely decline to answer and point out that, much as you would like to oblige, you might get in trouble or lose your job for violating the code of ethics. This response is also helpful when clients try to offer gifts or payment in gratitude for your services, something which is very hard to refuse in many cultures but is a clear breach of the interpreter's code of ethics.

Should I disqualify myself from a court case if I interpreted during the police investigation?

As a professional interpreter, there is no inherent conflict of interest if you interpret for law enforcement agencies as well as the defence; you should be able to remain impartial regardless of who has hired you to interpret. On the other hand, there may be a perception of bias in the defendant's eyes if, for example, you interpreted the police interrogation when he was arrested and then you show up to interpret in the consultation with his lawyer. He may feel that you are prejudiced against him, or will reveal information to the prosecution. In this case, full disclosure is the answer. You can inform all parties of your prior involvement in the case and allow them to decide whether they wish to continue using your services.

The judges and lawyers usually know nothing about my people. How can I educate them to avoid cultural misunderstandings while remaining impartial and unobtrusive?

While it is not appropriate for you to intervene in the proceedings to provide extensive explanations or clarifications of a cultural nature, there are other opportunities to educate legal professionals. On a personal level, you can contact the defence attorney or the prosecutor before going to court and warn them of any potential problems, or request permission to speak with the judge before the case begins. You can recommend some books or articles for them to read, or some cultural experts who might be consulted. Be careful not to provide information to one party that the other does not have access to, however, as you would lose your impartiality. An example of information that could legitimately be provided to one side only, most likely during preparation for testimony, would be the fact that nodding the head does not signify understanding in the defendant's or witness's culture. An example of information that should be shared with both defence and prosecution would be the identity of a professor of cultural anthropology who could provide information about marital customs in the defendant's or victim's culture.

Another way to educate legal professionals that protects the impartiality of individual interpreters is for an interpreters' association or an ethnic advocacy group to present workshops for judges and lawyers to promote cross-cultural understanding. The judges and lawyers, in turn, could be invited to address community groups to educate them about the justice system.

Conclusion

Developing and enforcing a code of professional conduct is a very complex process. Although court interpreting has been practised for centuries, only recently have legislators, jurists, and practitioners begun to examine the role of the interpreter in the courtroom and codify standards of performance. This effort is more advanced in some countries than in others, and even in jurisdictions where interpreters and legal professionals are well trained in proper procedure, solutions to ethical problems are not always clear-cut. There are still many courts throughout the world where very little thought has been given to the consequences of inappropriate behaviour in interpreted cases. Therefore, individual interpreters who attempt to adhere to strict standards may encounter resistance from legal professionals or colleagues who are reluctant to change their ways. The ethical principles presented here are ideal norms that all interpreters should strive to uphold, but the realities of day-to-day life in the justice system cannot be ignored.

Morris (1995 a & b), Niska (1995), and Mikkelson (1998) have examined the problems inherent in a profession whose standards are imposed by another, more powerful one (the legal profession) rather than being allowed to develop its own. Moeketsi (1999b:14) also points out that interpreters operate under very difficult circumstances in systems where the imbalance of power between court personnel and defendants is particularly acute. In South Africa, she reports, interpreters often feel compelled to take action that would be considered unethical in another context. She cites the case of an interpreter who renders the magistrate's simple question "Do you have a lawyer" as "Do you have a legal representative? This court allows you to seek your own lawyer. If you do not have money, you can use the lawyers paid for by the state". Her analysis (1999b:14):

> Here, the court interpreter added information to the magistrate's question. Much as [sic] his experience tells him that defendants are skeptic of State Legal Aid because they find it hard to reconcile the fact that the state wants to prosecute them on the one hand and provides them with defence attorneys on the other. The court interpreter knows that the magistrate's neglect to communicate that vital information is an irregularity that could lead to miscarriage of justice. Is he therefore expected to behave like a so-called conduit and transfer only the source message to the listener in the target language, or should he rather take it upon himself to rectify the obviously unacceptable situation and supply the crucial information and thereby save the magistrate from dereliction of duty, protect the accused from an unfair trial and ensure that criminal proceedings are conducted accordingly?

This chapter thus ends with a question, a reflection of the uncertainties that still prevail in the theory and practice of court interpreting.

Role-Playing Scenarios

Directions: Act out the following scenarios with your fellow students and explore different solutions to the problems posed.

A. You are interpreting in an interview between a defence attorney and his client, an elderly gentleman. The attorney calls the man by his first name and generally treats him in a casual, familiar way that is considered unacceptable in the defendant's culture. The defendant says to you, "I don't like this lawyer's attitude. Don't you think I should get another lawyer?"

B. You are interpreting at a sentencing, and it is clear to you that the defendant is intoxicated: he has a strong odour of alcohol on his breath, and he has trouble maintaining his balance. The judge asks the defendant a series of questions to determine whether he is ready to proceed. In re-

sponse to the question "Are you taking medication or under the influence of any substance that would impair your judgement?" the defendant
answers no. The defence attorney says nothing.

C. At a sentencing hearing, the judge imposes a stiff sentence on the defendant and declares the court in recess. As everyone is leaving the
courtroom, the defendant whispers to you that he is going to take his
revenge on the judge.

D. During your pre-testimony briefing of a prosecution witness, she con-
fides to you that a member of the defendant's family has contacted her
and threatened that if she doesn't change her testimony, she will suffer
grave consequences.

E. You are interpreting in a criminal case for a defendant for whom you
have previously interpreted in a mental hospital. You know from your
earlier assignment that he has been diagnosed with schizophrenia and
must take medication daily. He is being held in custody and has not been
taking the medication. The defence counsel is not aware of his medical
history.

Suggestions for Further Reading

The following books and articles contain interesting discussions of ethical
issues:

Colin, Joan and Ruth Morris (1996) *Interpreters and the Legal Process*, Winchester: Waterside Press.

Cooke, Michael (1995) 'Understood by All Concerned? Anglo/Aboriginal Legal
Translation', in M. Morris (ed) *Translation and the Law*, American Translators
Association Scholarly Monograph Series, Vol. VIII, Amsterdam & Philadelphia:
John Benjamins, 37-63.

Corsellis, Ann (1995) *Non-English Speakers and the English Legal System*, Cambridge: The Institute of Criminology, University of Cambridge, Cropwood
Occasional Paper No. 20.

De Jongh, Elena (1992) *An Introduction to Court Interpreting: Theory and Practice*, Lanham, MD: University Press of America.

Edwards, Alicia (1995) *The Practice of Court Interpreting*, Amsterdam & Philadelphia: John Benjamins.

González, Roseann, Victoria Vásquez and Holly Mikkelson (1991) *Fundamentals
of Court Interpretation: Theory, Policy and Practice*, Durham, North Carolina:
Carolina Academic Press.

Hale, Sandra and Cesar Luzardo (1997) 'What Am I Expected to Do? The Interpreter's Ethical Dilemma, a Study of Arabic, Spanish and Vietnamese Speakers'
Perceptions and Expectations of Interpreters', *Antipodean, The Australian Translation Journal* 1:10-16.

Khoon, W. F. (1990) 'Court Interpreting in a Multiracial Society – the Malaysian Experience', in D. Bowen and M. Bowen (eds) *Interpreting – Yesterday, Today, and Tomorrow*, American Translators Association Scholarly Monograph Series, Volume IV, Binghamton, NY: State University of New York at Binghamton, 108-116.

Moeketsi, Rosemary (1999a) *Discourse in a Multilingual and Multicultural Courtroom: A Court Interpreter's Guide*, Pretoria: JL van Schaik.

------ (1999b) 'Redefining the Role of the South African Court Interpreter', *Proteus* 3(3-4):12-15.

Morris, Ruth (1995a) 'The Moral Dilemmas of Court Interpreting', *The Translator* 1(1):25-46.

------ (1995b) 'Pragmatism, Precept and Passions: The Attitudes of English-language Legal Systems to non-English Speakers', in M. Morris (ed) *Translation and the Law*, American Translators Association Scholarly Monograph Series, Volume VIII, Amsterdam & Philadelphia: John Benjamins, 263-279.

Niska, Helge (1995) 'Just Interpreting: Role Conflicts and Discourse Types in Court Interpreting', in M. Morris (ed) *Translation and the Law*, American Translators Association Scholarly Monograph Series, Volume VIII. Amsterdam & Philadelphia: John Benjamins, 293-316.

Tsuda, Mamoru (1997) 'Human Rights Problems of Foreigners in Japan's Criminal Justice System', *Migrationworld* 25(1-2):22-25.

Suggestions for Further Study

1. How would you answer the question posed by Rosemary Moeketsi in the citation at the end of this chapter? Give the reasons for your position.
2. Write a code of ethics that incorporates the particular characteristics of the language combination and the court system in which you will be working. Translate it into your working languages and discuss the ethical and linguistic problems that arise.
3. Think of a cultural issue that might arise in the course of your work, and explain how you would deal with it in a manner consistent with the ethical principles discussed in this chapter.
4. Discuss ways in which court interpreters in your country might educate legal professionals about cultural issues that are of importance to court proceedings.

---

[1] The following codes of ethics were consulted for this chapter: *Best Practice in Court Interpreting* and *Code of Conduct for Court Interpreters*, International Federation of Translators (FIT) Committee for Legal Translators and Court Interpreters; *Code of Practice*, Australian Institute of Interpreters and Translators (AUSIT); *National Register of Public Service Interpreters' Code of Conduct; Model Code of Professional Responsibility for Interpreters in the Judiciary*, National Center for State Courts; *The RID Code of Ethics*, Registry of Interpreters for the Deaf; *Ehrenkodex*, Austrian Association of Court Interpreters.

6.   Interpreting Techniques

> A word is not a crystal, transparent and unchanged, it is the skin of a living thought and may vary greatly in colour and content according to the circumstances and the time in which it is used.
>
> Justice Oliver Wendell Holmes (1918; in Mellinkoff 1963:440)

> Of course I want counsel. But it is even more important to have a good interpreter.
>
> Hermann Göring (*Time*, 29 October 1945:38)

Ask a layperson about the work of the court interpreter and, to the extent that he has any idea at all what court interpreters do, his answer will probably focus on knowledge of a foreign language and of legal terms. Ask a judge or lawyer, and the answer will emphasize that interpreters must translate everything "verbatim", follow the law, and not interfere with the work of legal professionals. Stories in the press about interpreted trials often focus on miscarriages of justice due to incompetent interpreters, and the limited academic research that has been conducted in the field of judiciary interpreting also tends to put the spotlight on interpreter error (Berk-Seligson 1990, 1999; Hale 1997, 1999; Rigney 1999). Much of the discussion of court interpreting, including the preceding chapters in this book, examines the phenomenon externally, looking at the behaviour of the interpreter with respect to other actors in the courtroom and society at large. In this chapter we will shift the emphasis to the internal aspects of the legal interpreter's work, the nuts and bolts, if you will. After defining interpreting in general, we will examine each of the three modes of interpreting in detail as they are practised in the judiciary setting, and will then look at some of the ancillary tasks that court interpreters are often called upon to perform. The chapter will conclude with some practical exercises designed to enhance interpreting skills.

Definition of Interpreting

Briefly, **interpreting** is the transfer of an oral message from one language to another in real time (as opposed to **translating**, which is the transfer of a written message from one language to another and may take place years after the original message is written; note that the term **translation** is also often used to denote the overall process of interlingual meaning transfer, regardless of whether it is written or oral). In the case of sign language, interpreting involves transferring a message from an oral mode to a visual mode or vice-versa, also in real time. This seemingly simple process is complicated by the fact that it is difficult to define all of the elements that make up a message, and to transfer all of those elements intact from the **source language** (the language of the original message) to the **target language** (the language into which the message is being interpreted or translated). In his book *Translation and Translating: Theory and Practice* (1991), Roger T. Bell cites a standard definition of translation as "the replacement of a representation of a text in one language by a representation of an equivalent text in a second language", but goes on to explain that the matter of equivalence is exceedingly complex:

> Texts in different languages can be equivalent in different degrees (fully or partially equivalent), in respect of different levels of presentation (equivalent in respect of context, of semantics, of grammar, of lexis, etc.) and at different ranks (word-for-word, phrase-for-phrase, sentence-for-sentence). (Hartmann and Stork 1972, quoted in Bell 1991:6)

Bell then concludes that "the ideal of total equivalence is a chimera" (1991:6). Gile (1995:49) attributes the problem to the fact that "languages are not isomorphic":

> [I]n other words, there is no one-to-one correspondence between them as regards lexical elements ("words") or linguistic structures associated with rules of grammar, stylistic rules, etc. In particular, there is no automatic equivalence between words in the source and target languages, and apparently similar structures may have different uses and different connotations.

The issue of accuracy or fidelity in translation and interpretation has been addressed extensively and masterfully in other works (most notably in Catford 1965; Seleskovitch 1968; Nida and Taber 1974; Wilss 1982; Bell 1991; and Gile 1995). The broadly accepted standard is that interpreters should strive to retain every element of the source-language message in the target-language version, including not only lexical content, but also style, tone, and nuance. In his book on conference interpreting, Jones (1998:4-5) stresses that "interpreters must bridge the cultural and conceptual gaps" in addition to the purely linguistic ones that separate speakers of different languages, and may deviate from the letter of the original "only if it enhances the audience's understanding of the speaker's meaning".

What do interpreters need to know in order to bridge these gaps? According to Bell (1991:17), linguistics experts have identified different types of knowledge that go into language use:

> knowledge of the options available for (1) converting amorphous 'ideas' into concepts which are organized into propositions (semantic knowledge), (2) mapping propositions, which are universal and not tied to any

language, onto the clause-creating systems of a particular language (syntactic knowledge) and (3) realizing clauses as utterances and texts in actual communicative situations (rhetorical knowledge).

In addition to this linguistic competence, interpreters also need to develop "communicative competence", which is defined as

> the knowledge and ability possessed by the translator [and interpreter] which permits him/her to create communicative acts – discourse – which are not only (and not necessarily) grammatical but ... socially appropriate. (Hymes 1972, quoted in Bell 1991:42)

With regard to the judicial setting in particular, González et al (1991:16) emphasize that

> the court interpreter is required to interpret the original source material without editing, summarizing, deleting, or adding while conserving the language level, style, tone, and intent of the speaker or to render what may be termed the **legal equivalence** of the source message. (emphasis in original)

In this setting, the interpreter faces far more constraints than colleagues in other spheres, where guaranteeing the audience's understanding of the message is an essential part of the interpreter's role. The court interpreter's function is not necessarily to ensure understanding, but rather to put the target-language audience on an equal footing with speakers of the source language, who themselves may not fully understand the language of the court. Thus, the interpreter in court does not have as much latitude for explaining, clarifying, or adapting the message as she would in a business meeting or a diplomatic encounter.

The unique demands on the court interpreter will be discussed in more detail in the context of the specific modes of interpreting that are practised in the judicial setting. In addition to the modes into which interpreting is usually classified, namely, consecutive interpretation, simultaneous interpretation, and sight translation, another classification of interpreting has been established for the judiciary sphere. Hewitt (1995:34), who is writing about the United States, where English is the language of the courts, defines these categories as follows:

> **Proceedings interpretation** is for a non-English speaking litigant in order to make the litigant "present" and able to participate effectively during the proceeding. This interpreting function is ordinarily performed in the simultaneous mode. The interpreter's speech is always in the foreign language, and is not part of the record of the proceedings.
> **Witness interpretation** is interpretation during witness testimony for

the purpose of presenting evidence to the court. This interpreting function is performed in the consecutive mode; the English language portions
of the interpretation are part of the record of the proceeding. A variant of
"witness" interpreting is assistance provided by the interpreter during
communications between the judge or other English-speaking official on
the case and a non-English-speaking defendant or civil litigant. Typical
examples are communications who [sic] occur during arraignments, plea
or sentencing hearings.

Interview interpreting is interpreting to facilitate communication in interview or consultation settings. Interview interpreting may occur in
conjunction with court proceedings or before or after court proceedings.
Foremost among these are interviews or consultations that take place
between attorney and client (sometimes referred to as "defence" interpreting) and between a non-English speaking person and bail screening
or probation personnel. Interview interpreting may be performed in either or both the simultaneous and consecutive modes ... depending on
the circumstances.

Consecutive Interpreting

In **consecutive** interpreting, according to Jones (1998:5), "the interpreter lis-
tens to the totality of a speaker's comments, or at least a significant passage,
and then reconstitutes the speech with the help of notes taken while listening".
Because the interpreter must wait for the speaker to finish before beginning the
interpretation, consecutive interpreting adds considerably to the length of a proceeding. It is therefore considered more appropriate for witness testimony than
for proceedings, when all of the speakers share the same language and do not
like to stop and wait for the interpretation. Consecutive interpretation is used
for proceedings in many countries where a verbatim record is not kept but evidence is summarized. For example, in Japan, the judge, prosecutor, and defence
attorney each summarize the case from their point of view, and the interpreter
is expected to provide a consecutive interpretation for the defendant. This
style of consecutive interpreting, sometimes known as **long consecutive**, is
similar to that practised by conference interpreters, and is appropriate only
for tightly controlled sessions in which the parties patiently wait for each utterance to be interpreted.

   In the common-law criminal trial, which as we have seen is often characterized by rapid-fire questioning of witnesses and occasional emotional outbursts,
long consecutive interpreting is not feasible. Instead, interpreters practise **short**
or **sequential consecutive interpreting** of witness testimony, which operates
at the sentence level instead of working with paragraphs or entire speeches (De
Jongh 1992:38). The questions are posed in the official language of the court
and then interpreted into the witness's language; the witness responds in the

foreign language, and that response is interpreted back into the language of the court for the official record. When interpreting into the witness's language, the interpreter has an audience of just one person, and can speak *sotto voce* unless one of the participants has asked to monitor the interpretation. When interpreting the witness's answers into the official language of the court for the record, the interpreter must speak loudly enough to be heard by everyone in the courtroom.

Much has been written about the so-called "verbatim requirement" that prevails in court interpreting (González et al 1991; Morris 1995a & b; Mikkelson 1998), which has been imposed on interpreters by misguided judges and lawyers. Although the latter often instruct interpreters to "translate word for word" (Morris 1995) exactly what the witness says, it is clear to anyone who speaks more than one language that such a translation would render the message meaningless in the target language. What is really meant by a "verbatim" interpretation is that every single element of meaning in the source-language message must be accounted for in the target-language version. In the words of González et al (1991:16):

> The interpreter is required to render in a **verbatim manner** the form and content of the linguistic and paralinguistic elements of a discourse, including all of the pauses, hedges, self-corrections, hesitations, and emotion as they are conveyed through tone of voice, word choice, and intonation ... (emphasis in original)

This has profound implications for the training of court interpreters. The way consecutive interpreting is practised by conference interpreters, hedges, self-corrections, and hesitations are omitted, resulting in a more concise rendition that is sometimes more polished and better organized than the original (Weber 1984:49-50). This approach actually makes the interpreter's job somewhat easier, because she is free to concentrate on the speaker's ideas without being distracted by the paralinguistic elements of the message. A skilled conference interpreter can deal with "any length of speech" under these circumstances (Jones 1998:5). Because the interpretation of a witness's testimony must mirror the original utterance as closely as possible so that the triers of fact can assess the person's credibility, the court interpreter must burden her short-term memory with these additional elements. Consequently, a skilled court interpreter cannot be expected to retain more than 100 words (one or two sentences) before intervening to interpret. Fortunately, testifying witnesses are rarely given the opportunity to speak any longer than that, because attorneys want to maintain control over their statements.

The ability to coordinate speaker turn-taking is therefore an essential skill that all court interpreters must master. Deciding when to intervene in a lengthy statement is a critical judgement based on the interpreter's assessment of her own memory capacity, the witness's speaking style, and the impact an interpreter interruption will have on the witness's perceived credibility. Berk-Seligson (1990) has analyzed the impact of the interpreter on witness credibility with reference to O'Barr's (1982) research on powerful and powerless speech in the courtroom, and she has found that witnesses who are interrupted every few words by the interpreter are perceived as less credible than those who are allowed to speak at their own pace. The interpreter must thus weigh the risk of altering perceptions of the witness against the risk of failing to interpret accurately, and act accordingly.

As noted above, the consecutive interpreting practised in the courtroom tends to operate at the level of sentences or phrases. As a result, the notetaking techniques that are taught in interpreting schools where long consecutive is emphasized must be adapted for court interpreting to take into account the unique requirements. Some court interpreters do make use of the symbols representing key concepts, the notion of verticalization and indentation, the arrows and lines, and other features of consecutive notetaking developed by conference interpreters (Rozan 1956). An informal survey of prastising court interpreters in the United States revealed, however, that most take notes only on names and numbers (Mikkelson, Vásquez and González 1989). The interpreters reported that they avoid elaborate notetaking because it requires losing eye contact with the witness, which they consider vital to exerting situational control. They always like to have a notepad and pen available, however, even if they take few notes.

The component skills required for consecutive interpreting can be broken down into three categories: lexical, communication, and retention skills. Lexical skills include familiarity with the legal register of the courtroom (especially the questioning style of trial lawyers), the characteristic registers of lay witnesses and defendants (colloquial, conversational speech, street slang, and the argot of the underworld) and the technical jargon used by expert witnesses (law enforcement personnel, criminalists, medical professionals, and scientists). Communication skills include voice projection and modulation, coordination of turn-taking, and familiarity with courtroom protocol. Retention skills encompass active listening, mnemonic techniques, and notetaking.

Simultaneous Interpreting

In **simultaneous** interpreting, according to Gaiba (1998:16),

> the information is transferred into the second language as soon as interpreters understand a "unit" of meaning. The word "simultaneous" is misleading, because interpreters have to understand a minimum of information before they can translate into the target language. The lag

between the original and the interpreted version is called *décalage,* and
its length varies according to the interpreters. It is usually no longer than
seven or eight seconds.

The Nuremburg War Crimes Trial of 1945-46 is generally recognized as the
first instance of the use of electronic equipment to make possible simultaneous
interpretation of proceedings in multiple languages. Simultaneous interpreting
equipment has become quite sophisticated, and it is now taken for granted that
international meetings can be conducted efficiently with multiple working languages. Gaiba points out in her book about the Nuremburg Trial, however, that
interpreting with such equipment is "seldom used in courts because of its cost
to the government", and that the norm is whispered interpreting or *chuchotage.*
In this method, "interpreters sit next to the people who do not understand the
working language and whisper the translation in their ears" (Gaiba 1998:16).

In the United States, many interpreters are using wireless equipment to enable them to speak into a microphone at a very low volume and be heard clearly
by a defendant wearing earphones, even at a distance of several yards. Although this expedient is not as appropriate as the soundproof booths and
high-technology equipment used for conference interpreting, it does allow the
interpreter to position herself adequately so as to see and hear all participants,
protect her voice, and avoid the strain of leaning in to whisper directly in the
defendant's ear (Grusky 1988; Edwards 1995). Sometimes interpreters will com-
bine simultaneous and consecutive interpreting for witness testimony, with
questions being interpreted simultaneously for the witness alone to hear, and
answers being interpreted consecutively in a loud enough voice for the entire
courtroom to hear.

Unfortunately, even simultaneous interpreting without equipment, which
creates more of a strain for the interpreter, is not the norm in courts everywhere.
Due to the lack of trained interpreters and the ignorance of court personnel,
many interpreted proceedings are conducted with summary consecutive interpretation (Tsuda 1995; De Mas 1999; Rivezzi 1999). It is widely agreed that
simultaneous interpretation is really the only acceptable mode of interpreting to
keep the defendant informed of what is happening in the proceedings, and that
court systems should make a greater effort to recruit trained interpreters who
can demonstrate proficiency in simultaneous interpretation (Driesen 1988, 1989;
González et al 1991; Hewitt 1995; Nicholson and Martinsen 1997).

Simultaneous interpretation is a complex task that requires extensive training, and even skilled simultaneous interpreters make errors if they work under
inadequate conditions. The interpreter needs to be able to see and hear the speaker
clearly in order to render an accurate interpretation, and the speaker's rate of
speech must be reasonable (Jones 1998). Furthermore, frequent breaks should
be allowed to prevent interpreter fatigue (González et al 1991). Studies have

shown that even experienced conference interpreters begin to make errors after 20 or 30 minutes of simultaneous interpreting, and it is therefore recommended that for proceedings that will last longer than that period, interpreters should work in pairs so that they can relieve each other frequently (Vidal 1997). Many courts will find this standard impossible to meet, given that there may be few or no qualified interpreters in some language combinations, but as the court interpreting profession becomes more widely recognized, training and working conditions will improve, and the courts will be better able to ensure due process for litigants who do not speak the official language of the legal system.

We have already noted that languages are not isomorphic, and therefore interpreters must "repackage" the message to make it understandable in the target language. This task is much more difficult in simultaneous interpretation because of the time factor. When interpreting from a source language that is characterized by a subject-object-verb (SOV) syntax into a target language that follows a subject-verb-object (SVO) order, for example, the interpreter must often wait several seconds to hear the verb before rendering the message in the target language in the appropriate order. This waiting time is the *décalage* mentioned by Gaiba (1998), and is one of the most important strategies interpreters must learn. It takes a lot of concentration to lag behind the speaker long enough to restructure the message without forgetting any elements of meaning; Jones (1998:74) calls this "cultivating split attention". He also points out that the degree to which the interpreter lags behind the speaker varies tremendously depending on the syntax of the languages in question and the information available to the interpreter. The exercises listed at the end of this chapter are helpful for enhancing concentration and expanding *décalage*.

To wait for a key element such as the verb without long pauses, sometimes interpreters use "neutral" or "filler" phrases to "buy time" until they have enough information to complete the thought, while avoiding phrases that commit them grammatically or semantically to a certain meaning. Gaiba (1998:104) describes the strategy devised by the interpreters at Nuremburg for coping with long, convoluted German sentences in which the verb came at the end:

> [T]hey started the sentence with vague and general phrases and then became more specific once they heard the verb. This allowed them to keep pace with the speaker and to deliver a reasonable, even if not elegant, translation.

For example, a judge may say:

> You have the right to have a misdemeanor or felony charge against you dismissed if you are not tried within the statutory period of time.

The interpreter recognizes that the verb "to have" is likely to be an auxiliary in a split verb phrase ("to have [the charge] dismissed") and holds the initial phrase in short-term memory until she has enough information. The interpreted version, back-translated into English, would be as follows:

> With respect to a misdemeanor or felony charge, if you are not tried within the statutory period of time you have a right to a dismissal of the charge.

Another strategy often employed by simultaneous interpreters is *anticipation*, whereby the interpreter applies her knowledge of the subject matter, patterns of usage in the source language, the speaker's style, and the context of the speech to predict what the speaker will say without having to wait for a key element such as the verb. This is a risky practice that requires a lot of experience to master. As Gaiba (1998:104) points out, it requires "native-like knowledge" of the source language. In the case of English, in which adjectives tend to precede the noun they are describing, and speakers will often reel off a whole string of adjectives before getting around to the all-important noun, an interpreter may need to restructure the message to put the noun before the adjectives in the target language. It may be possible for her to anticipate the noun based on the initial adjectives and the context of the speech. For example, an attorney may address the jury in a closing argument with this statement:

> Ladies and gentlemen of the jury, I submit to you that this is the most heinous, despicable, outrageous, unconscionable crime ever committed against a child.

The interpreter can safely predict the noun after hearing "heinous," which is a relatively rare word that almost always appears in a collocation with "crime". To be safe, however, she might use a more neutral term like "act" instead of "crime".

In languages with radically different syntaxes, interpreters may have to resort to more drastic restructuring. This technique is known as "salami" among conference interpreters, and Jones (1998:103) cites an example of a German-to-English interpretation in which this strategy is applied. The original German statement, translated literally into English, is:

> We have tried with the photographer, who the man [accusative case], who on the scene of this serious accident was seen, as he to the injured assistance brought, had identified, to get into contact.

The interpreter turns the many dependent clauses into short sentences that stand alone:

> A man was seen at this serious accident. He was helping the injured. He has been identified by a photographer. We have tried to get into contact with the photographer.

Thus, to perform simultaneous interpretation efficiently and accurately, interpreters must develop a number of component skills. In addition to the lexical, communication, and retention skills identified as important for consecutive interpretation, simultaneous interpreters must possess 1) quick reflexes and mental agility for rapid restructuring of messages, 2) the ability to monitor their own output while also attending carefully to the speaker to make sure they are producing an accurate and intelligible target-language message, and 3) the stamina necessary to cope with the stress inherent in simultaneous interpreting.

Sight Translation

Sight translation is the oral translation of a written document. It is necessary when standard legal forms must be signed by litigants who do not speak the language of the court, or when documents written in a foreign language are submitted as evidence. Because the interpreter has little time to study the document and prepare to render it orally in the target language, sight translation is not appropriate for lengthy, technical reports or briefs. Particularly in countries where much of the evidence submitted to court is in written form, documents should be translated by professionals who are given adequate time for research and production of a polished translation. In the case of a standard form that an interpreter can become familiar with in advance, or a short document like a birth certificate that is used to prove a defendant's age, sight translation is an appropriate expedient.

González et al (1991:401) describe the process in this way:

> Sight translation is analogous to sight reading in music: the interpreter is given a [source language] document never seen before, and, with minimal preparation, the interpreter provides a complete oral translation of the document into the [target language]. Like accomplished musicians who play an apparently effortless version of a piece they have never laid eyes on, interpreters are actually drawing upon years of training and experience to perform this feat. The end product should be both faithful to the original text and pleasing to the ear (that is, in free-flowing, natural-sounding language).

The mental process of sight translation is very similar to that of simultaneous interpretation, except that the source message is in written rather than oral form. Consequently, the same component skills that go into simultaneous interpreting, i.e., quick reflexes and mental agility, plus the ability to monitor one's own output while carefully attending to the original, are required for sight translation. In addition, the interpreter must be able to grasp the meaning of a written text quickly and then convert a message that was originally intended to be read into one that can be understood in oral form. This may involve breaking up long, convoluted sentences into shorter, more direct statements, as well as using stress and intonation to clarify meaning. Interpreters must therefore be familiar with both the oral and written forms of their working languages, which sometimes differ greatly.

An added difficulty arises when handwritten documents are presented to the court as evidence, such as when a defendant writes a letter to the judge for the sentencing hearing, or correspondence between two individuals is introduced as evidence in a conspiracy case. Often the writers of such documents are not well-versed in the rules of grammar and punctuation in their native language – indeed, they may be putting in written form a language that does not even have an official orthography, as in the case of indigenous languages that have never been written down – and the interpreter may have difficulty deciphering the handwriting and understanding the intended meaning of the document. One strategy for coping with this problem is to read the document out loud before attempting to translate it, as writers are often simply transcribing the way they actually talk in conversation.

Ancillary Tasks

In addition to interpreting and sight translating documents in court, judiciary interpreters are sometimes called upon to perform related tasks. As stated earlier, written materials requiring translation are frequently submitted to the court, and court personnel may assume that interpreters will be able to translate them. In fact, translating and interpreting, while closely related, are different skills that not everyone is capable of mastering equally; in other words, some individuals possessing the prerequisite linguistic skills are better at translating than interpreting, and vice-versa. Unfortunately, however, laypersons are often unaware of this distinction. Moreover, legal translation is a highly specialized field within the translation profession, and many of the documents involved in court cases require the expertise of trained legal translators who are familiar with different legal systems and the conventions of legal documentation. In many countries, the law requires that all translations be produced by professionals who are legally authorized to use the title "sworn translator" or "public translator". In any case, it is important for interpreters to candidly assess their translation ability and to turn down translation assignments if they feel they cannot perform the task adequately.

Gile (1995:71) uses the metaphor of road signs pointing to a destination to illustrate the difference between oral and written language, and thus between translating and interpreting:

... when writing a text, Senders have time to select the signs and place them carefully along the route, changing them until they are satisfied. When making speeches, Senders focus on the destination and tend to grab whatever signs are available at the time they believe they are necessary. When reading a translation, Receivers have time to stop and look at the signs along the way and note a particular selection or arrangement of signs. In interpretation, they travel at high speed and have less time to do so. This means that it can be important for *translators* to be able to select and place their target-language signs carefully so as to lead Receivers in a way closely resembling the one selected for them by the Sender; for *interpreters*, it is more important to be able to drive rapidly to their destination, following Speakers at their own speed, while also selecting and placing their own signs at the same time ... (emphasis in original)

Another task that court interpreters are being asked to perform with increasing frequency is the transcription and translation of recorded conversations, obtained through tapped phone lines or secret recordings made by undercover agents. In their books on court interpreting, González et al (1991) and Edwards (1995) each devote an entire chapter to tape transcription and translation, an indication of the complexity of this highly specialized task. Like sight translation, tape transcription involves both oral and written language, and the contrasts noted above must be taken into consideration. Furthermore, conversations involving criminal acts are even more cryptic and ambiguous than ordinary conversations between two people who share a great deal of background knowledge, making translation even more difficult. Edwards (1995) and other interpreters with experience in tape transcription and translation recommend the following guidelines:

1. Try to obtain the original recording rather than copies, because sound quality is extremely important for accuracy.
2. Use proper transcribing equipment, including earphones, foot controls, and features that enable you to slow down the tape and enhance the sound.
3. Transcribing tapes, especially those of poor quality, such as those obtained from body wires on undercover agents, is extremely time-consuming. Therefore, allow sufficient time to complete the assignment in a satisfactory manner. Transcribing poor quality recordings may require up to one hour for each minute of recorded material. Services should be billed by the hour.
4. Listen to the entire recording at least three times before attempting to transcribe it, to make sure you know the context and are familiar with the speakers' voices, accents, and vocabulary.
5. Everything you hear should be transcribed, including nonverbal utterances, pauses, and background noise. Overlapping speech and

unintelligible portions should also be noted. Some indication of the length of pauses and the size of unintelligible segments should be given by means of dots, hyphens, or some other symbol representing the passage of time or the number of syllables. The transcript should be accompanied by a key indicating the meaning of these symbols.

6. Do not attempt to identify parties by name unless specifically instructed to do so. It is preferable to use labels such as Male Voice 1, Male Voice 2, etc.

7. After completing the transcription, begin the translation. It should be inserted next to the original in a side-by-side, two-column format so that the reader can compare the two easily.

8. Conversations recorded surreptitiously in undercover investigations are often characterized by deliberately vague language and code words. Keep the translation as vague as the original in order to avoid prejudicing the reader. For example, if a speaker says, "The merchandise is ready for pickup", do not say, "The drugs are ready for pickup", even though you know that is what he is referring to.

9. Any comments you feel are necessary to point out ambiguities (e.g., "he/she/it" when subject pronouns are not specified), describe sounds ("cough", "phone ringing"), or indicate unintelligibility should be clearly marked with square brackets so that they will not be mistaken for words uttered by the speakers. Sometimes translator's footnotes may be necessary for lengthy explanations.

10. Fragments of words in the original should be rendered with fragments of words in the translation whenever possible (e.g., "jue-" in the transcription of a conversation in Spanish can be rendered as "Thur-" in the English translation, if the translator has enough context to know that the speaker is talking about days of the week). If the meaning of the fragment is not clear, that should be noted as well.

11. When the transcription and translation are complete, they should be reviewed by another interpreter for quality control. Remember that you may be called to testify as an expert witness on the transcription, so you must be able to defend your work.

12. The identity of the transcriber(s) and translator(s) and their credentials should be included in a statement at the end of the document. The equipment used for the transcription should also be noted. A typical statement would read: "I, Holly Mikkelson, certified as a court interpreter by the Administrative Office of the U.S. Courts and accredited as a translator by the American Translators Association, do hereby declare that I prepared the foregoing transcription and translation to the best of my ability, based on what I was able to hear using a Sony 9000 transcribing machine".

Remote Interpreting

As communications technology improves, physical distance is no longer considered a barrier to communication. Consequently, with increasing frequency interpreters are being asked to provide services to parties who are not in the same room, city, or even country. Telephone and video-conference interpreting are becoming an attractive option for court administrators who want to save travel costs, gain access to qualified interpreters in rare languages, and enhance security (especially in the case of criminal defendants who are in custody). These are all valid considerations, although the savings in time and money are not always as great as originally envisioned. Even more important, however, are the disadvantages of impeded communication. It is widely recognized that interpreters must see the faces of the speakers they are interpreting in order to receive both the linguistic and paralinguistic aspects of the source message as reliably as possible (Seleskovitch 1968; Jones 1998). In telephone interpreting, not only does the interpreter lose the vital information that can be obtained from observing the speakers' body language, but it is also much more difficult for her to exert the situational control required to manage turn-taking in consecutive interpreting (which is still the usual mode for over-the-phone interpreting, though improved technology will soon make simultaneous interpretation more feasible).

Telephone and video-conference interpreting have improved access to interpreting services in places like Australia and the United States, where distances are vast and the diversity of languages is great (Heh and Qian 1997; Ozolins 1998). Even proponents of this method acknowledge, however, that it is not suitable for all kinds of proceedings, and should be limited to short and simple transactions such as setting dates. Certainly a remote interpreter is preferable to a live interpreter who is incompetent or biased, or no interpreter at all. But given the complexity of court proceedings and the high stakes involved, due process cannot be fully guaranteed unless the interpreter is allowed to work under optimum conditions (Vidal 1998).

Practical Exercises

The following exercises are designed to be performed in a single language (e.g., repeating an English speech in English, or reading a Chinese text while listening to a recorded passage in Chinese). Do not attempt to interpret between languages. Try doing these exercises in all of your working languages. Always record your practice sessions and play back what you have done so that you can critique yourself and make improvements.

Active Listening and Retention

1. Obtain an audio or video tape of a presentation on a technical subject, such as instructions for repairing an appliance, or an explanation of a scientific process or concept. Listen to a segment of approximately five minutes without taking any notes, and then try to repeat the main ideas. Gradually increase the length of the segments you try to recall.

2. Repeat the preceding exercise, but as you listen, jot down key words to remind yourself of the main ideas. Then repeat as much as you recall. Gradually increase the length of the segments you try to recall. Compare the results you obtain with and without notes.

3. Often we are unable to retain information because we disagree with the speaker, and we engage in a mental argument rather than listening attentively. This is a particular problem for court interpreters, who must interpret for individuals they may not like, or who they suspect may be lying. To improve your ability to listen attentively without interference from your own bias, obtain a recording of a speech on a controversial topic by a speaker with whom you disagree. After listening to the speech, try to repeat as much as you recall. State the ideas convincingly, as if you believed them.

4. To enhance your awareness of the non-verbal aspects of communication, watch a scene in a video recording of a movie or television programme in which the characters engage in dialogue, with the volume turned down. Try to guess what the conversation is about based only on what you observe. Then view the video with sound to check your assumptions.

5. Ask a friend or fellow student to describe in detail a recent incident, such as a shopping expedition, a trip to a nearby city, or an argument with a friend. Try to repeat the story verbatim. Compare your results with and without notes.

Communication Skills

1. Practise reading aloud a variety of texts, including narrative fiction, dialogue, news reports, and technical manuals. Record yourself and listen critically to your enunciation and intonation.

2. Give a speech on a controversial topic, defending a position with which you actually disagree (it helps to have an audience for this exercise).

Split Attention

1. Practise performing two unrelated tasks at the same time, such as repeating ("shadowing") a recorded speech while writing multiplication tables

or a favourite poem. Be sure to record yourself and listen critically to your enunciation and intonation. Gradually increase the speed and complexity of the recorded speeches (these can be obtained from the Internet, from international or national political organizations, or from schools for court reporters).
2. Read aloud a written passage (a magazine or newspaper article, for example, while listening to a recorded speech on an unrelated topic. Afterwards, give the main ideas of both the written passage and the recorded speech.

Restructuring

1. To enhance your linguistic flexibility, read aloud a speech or a passage from a magazine or newspaper, and as you go along try to change the wording without altering the meaning. For example, "the beginning of a new era" can be changed to "the dawn of a new age", and "the policeman was doubtful of the suspect's story" could be rephrased as "the version given by the detainee was received with skepticism by the law enforcement officer".
2. To further enhance your mental agility, repeat the preceding exercise, but with oral input (a recorded speech). The first time you hear the speech, you may not be able to rephrase very much, but as you repeat the exercise with the same speech, you will gradually find new and creative ways to state the same ideas in different words. This is a particularly useful exercise for your second language.
3. Practise paraphrasing both written and oral passages, as above, but make a conscious effort to alter the register, from formal to informal or vice-versa.
4. Paraphrase written and oral passages by stating the ideas more concisely. Repeat the exercise but state the ideas more verbosely.

Anticipation

1. Have a friend copy a passage from a newspaper or magazine and obliterate words or phrases throughout the text. The obliteration may be random (e.g., every five words), or meaning-based (e.g., all verbs). Then read the redacted passage aloud and try to fill in the missing words based on your knowledge of patterns of usage in the language and the context and subject matter of the passage.
2. Play a recorded speech and press the "pause" button every few seconds; then try to predict what the speaker will say next.

Interpreting

When you make the transition from these exercises to interpreting consecutively or simultaneously between languages, begin with recordings of relatively slow speeches or stories (100 to 120 words per minute) on general topics. Be sure to record your interpretation and listen to it critically, repeating each speech several times until you are satisfied with your interpretation. Gradually increase the speed and complexity of the material you interpret.

Suggestions for Further Reading

The following works are particularly useful for learning the pragmatic aspects of court interpreting:

De Jongh, Elena (1992) *An Introduction to Court Interpreting: Theory and Practice*, Lanham, MD: University Press of America.
Edwards, Alicia (1995) *The Practice of Court Interpreting*, Amsterdam & Philadelphia: John Benjamins.
Gile, Daniel (1995) *Basic Concepts and Models for Interpreter and Translator Training*, Amsterdam & Philadelphia: John Benjamins.
González, Roseann, Victoria Vásquez and Holly Mikkelson (1991) *Fundamentals of Court Interpretation: Theory, Policy and Practice*, Durham, North Carolina: Carolina Academic Press.
Ilg, Gérard and Sylvie Lambert (1996) 'Teaching Consecutive Interpreting', *Interpreting* 1(1): 69-99.
Jones, Roderick (1998) *Conference Interpreting Explained*, Manchester: St. Jerome.

Suggested Class Activities

1. Stage a mock trial with students playing the parts of defence counsel, defendant, prosecutor, judge, and witness.
2. Name an instance in which consecutive interpreting is more appropriate than simultaneous, and explain why.
3. Find a newspaper account of a criminal case and play the role of the defence counsel giving the final argument before the court, to be interpreted by the class.

7.   Specialized Topics, Resources and References

> The desire of knowledge, like the thirst of riches, increases ever with
> the acquisition of it.
>
> > Laurence Sterne (*Tristam Shandy*, 1759-67;
> > in Erlich & De Bruhl 1996:359)

In the preceding chapter we examined the interpreting process and the types of
linguistic and communicative competence that court interpreters must develop.
Now we will look at the content knowledge that is required for court interpreting. We have already seen in Chapter 3 that interpreters need to have some
understanding of criminal and civil procedure in the courts where they work
and in the countries where their languages are spoken. They also must be familiar with the evidence that is presented in typical criminal and civil cases, and
the associated terminology. In this chapter we will review the most common
criminal offences and civil-law issues that you are likely to encounter in your
work as a court interpreter. Then we will discuss the resources that are available
to help you research the subject matter and terminology related to these topics.
The chapter concludes with recommendations for continuing education.

Criminal Cases

Traffic: Even the most law-abiding citizen will at some time in his life come
into contact with law enforcement authorities in connection with a traffic viola-
tion. These offences are considered the least serious, and are often dealt with in
a separate court. Nonetheless, the evidence presented in traffic cases can be
quite technical, especially with respect to accidents and vehicle maintenance.
For instance, a truck driver may receive a citation for not having the required
safety equipment, or a police officer in a reckless driving case may present testimony about road conditions and signage. You must therefore know the correct
terms for all parts of passenger and freight vehicles, road signs, features of public roadways (e.g., *median strip, fast lane, overpass, double yellow line*), and
driving terms (e.g., *skid, swerve, pull over*).

Terms used by police officers in describing arrest procedures are also likely
to come up in testimony. Specific terms related to driving while intoxicated, an
offence which is being enforced with increasing vigour in many countries, are
also important. These include the symptoms of intoxication and the tests that
are administered to measure blood alcohol content. Because numbers are noto-
riously difficult to interpret accurately, you should prepare by learning the
numbers of frequently violated code sections. Obtaining copies of vehicle or

traffic codes in all of your working languages will help you not only with code sections, but also with terminology.

Controlled Substances: Drug abuse is a growing problem around the world, and you must be prepared to deal with evidence related to different illegal substances, how they are packaged, transported, sold, and consumed. You should be familiar with both the scientific names of the drugs and the names they are given on the street. Studying the laws governing controlled substances (usually the penal code or the health and safety code) will give you the scientific names and the appropriate terms for illegal drug paraphernalia. The drug subculture has a very elaborate language featuring many euphemisms and slang terms that will be repeated in testimony or heard in undercover recordings.

Law enforcement agents also have their own jargon for undercover operations (*stings* and *controlled buys*, for example) and arrests (*raids* and *busts*, for example). You may also encounter technical testimony about hazardous materials, equipment, and chemicals found in drug laboratories. Money laundering is a drug-related offence that has only recently been defined in the penal codes of many countries. It involves channeling the large amounts of cash generated by illicit transactions into legitimate businesses in order to conceal criminal activities from the authorities. Testimony in money laundering cases will include financial, banking, and business terms.

Property Crimes: Testimony in these cases can be very challenging for interpreters because of the wide variety of personal property that may be stolen, including electronic equipment, clothing, jewelry, furniture, appliances, and vehicles, as well as any item that could be taken from a commercial establishment (toys, lingerie, snacks – the possibilities are endless). Professional shoplifters and pickpockets use certain paraphernalia to aid them in their crimes, and burglars carry certain tools for breaking into homes and businesses. Testimony about burglary cases will usually include terms related to locks and security devices, as well as architectural terms (e.g., *window sill, doorframe, eaves*). In the case of auto burglary (not to be confused with car theft), auto parts will be mentioned frequently.

Weapons: Criminal activities often involve the use of firearms or other weapons. Certain weapons seem to be preferred in some cultures, and firearms are much more prevalent in some countries than others, so you should become familiar with the weapons most frequently used in the country where you work. Testimony about firearms will include not only the names of different guns (*pistol, revolver, rifle*), but also the way the gun is fired, how it may malfunction, and how it may be modified (such as converting a semiautomatic weapon to full automatic by filing down the sear pin). Different types of ammunition will be mentioned, and there may be evidence about ballistics tests to determine the identity of weapons or the origin of casings or slugs found at the crime scene. Testimony about knives will include the shape, size and colour of the handle and blade, as well as specialized features such as switchblades. If wounds are inflicted, there will be forensic evidence involving angles of incidence, entry and exit wounds, powder burns, slash marks, and the like.

Sex Offences: These cases are particularly stressful to interpret, because explicit testimony must be presented regarding the acts that were performed. Reliving the experience can be traumatic for the victim, and the interpreter must take special care not to become emotionally involved. Reading penal code sections related to sexual assault, rape, child molesting, sodomy, incest, and other sex offences will help you research related terminology in your working languages. It is also important to be familiar with the slang terms people use for body parts and sexual practices, as unsophisticated witnesses (especially children) may not know the appropriate clinical terms, or they may be asked to recount a conversation in which such language was used. Expert witness testimony in sex offence cases will deal with collecting evidence at the crime scene, giving the victim a medical exam, and testing substances such as bodily fluids, hair, and fibres. Recent developments in DNA profiling have resulted in sophisticated tests to determine the identity of perpetrators, and testimony about such evidence can be quite technical.

White Collar Crimes: These crimes, which derive their name from the fact that they are non-violent offences committed by people who are gainfully employed, tend to be financial in nature. In addition to money laundering, mentioned above, they include embezzlement, insider trading on the stock market, mail fraud, forgery, and larceny. As the Internet expands throughout the world, crimes committed in that medium will become more prevalent as well. In some countries, criminal charges may also be filed for acts such as sexual harassment or racial discrimination. Testimony in these cases can be very technical, dealing with complex regulations or sophisticated financial transactions.

Criminalistic Evidence: This kind of evidence can be presented in cases of any of the types mentioned above, as criminalists (who are not to be confused with criminologists, who specialize in the sociology of criminal behaviour) are scientists who apply their knowledge to any sort of criminal evidence. They usually work at crime labs, and specialize in fields such as accident reconstruction, ballistics, explosives, drugs, fibres, serology (the study of bodily fluids, including DNA profiling), chemistry, or fingerprints. A criminalist could testify about whether saliva found on a cigarette butt matches that of the defendant; whether the blood spatters found at the murder scene are consistent with eye-witness testimony about a physical altercation; whether the remnants of a match found at an arson site correspond to the matchbook found in the pocket of the defendant; or whether paint scrapings and tire tracks at an accident scene match those of a suspect vehicle. Interpreting such expert witness testimony for the defendant is challenging, and the best way to prepare for it is to request a copy of the criminalist's report before testimony begins.

Civil Cases

Divorce: Perhaps the most common type of civil case in which interpreters become involved is divorce. The laws governing divorce vary a great deal from one country to another, which means that the kinds of evidence produced vary as well. There may be testimony about adultery or abuse, about marital and domestic relations, or about property and financial matters. If there are children, matters of custody and visitation will be discussed. Evidence may be presented concerning childrearing practices, religious beliefs, and household expenses for purposes of determining spousal and child support payments.

Wills and Probate: Wills are complicated documents that cannot be translated without extensive preparation. If you are asked to interpret in a law office for someone who is drawing up a will, or for the reading of the will in the presence of the heirs, you should obtain the relevant documents ahead of time to prepare. The terminology will most likely involve real and personal property, bequests and charitable contributions, trusts, executors and administrators, types of heirs and beneficiaries, taxes, and standard legal phrases that appear in notarized documents (e.g., *in witness whereof, hereby attest*). If a will is being litigated in court for some reason, there may be testimony about family relationships and the mental and physical state of the decedent. It is helpful to study sections of the civil code regarding wills and succession to prepare for these cases.

Adoption: Evidence in these cases will focus on the prospective parents' financial status and domestic relations, as well as legal regulations governing adoption in the country in question. Issues such as parental rights and obligations, birth and death records, religious practices, and powers of attorney may arise as well.

Landlord-Tenant Relations: The most common type of case heard in court in this category is eviction, in which a property owner seeks the removal of a renter, usually for non-payment of rent. There will be testimony about the terms of the rental agreement, the condition of the dwelling (including plumbing, wiring, heating, leaky roofs, faulty appliances, etc.), and tenant behaviour (such as noise, cleanliness, number of residents, relations with neighbors, etc.). Sometimes a government agency will hold a hearing based on complaints about substandard housing or racial and ethnic discrimination.

Labour Relations: Civil litigation in the area of labour law may deal with union organizing activities, labour disputes, industrial accidents and job safety, unemployment insurance, sexual harassment, or racial and ethnic discrimination. To prepare for interpreting in such cases, you should talk to the parties and find out what the issues are so that you can obtain copies of contracts or regulations. Often there is very detailed testimony about the work itself, including machinery, materials, procedures, safety equipment, and the command structure of the workplace. A visit to the job site, if possible, is helpful for preparation.

Property Law: Evidence presented in these cases will include deeds, loan contracts, and other legal documents that require technical expertise to translate. Testimony may cover the terms of contracts and agreements, surveying boundaries, geographic features, environmental regulations, financial transactions, taxes, sewage and drainage, architecture and construction, and agricultural practices.

Business Law: In addition to the labour and property law cases mentioned above, other issues that may arise in litigation between businesses are contract enforcement, partnerships, insurance, investment, financial transactions (e.g., loans, bank accounts, stock offers, bond issues, dividends), accounting and bookkeeping, bankruptcy, product liability, bidding specifications, copyright and trademark violations, industrial secrets, and unfair competition. Clearly, business law is an extremely diverse and complex field, requiring a great deal of specialized knowledge on the part of translators and interpreters.

Resources for Research and Preparation

The novice interpreter who encounters an unknown term is likely to turn first to the most obvious resource, the bilingual dictionary. A few unpleasant experiences are usually enough to convince the interpreter that this is not always the wisest course of action. The meaning of a word may shift dramatically from one context to another, so interpreters cannot necessarily rely on dictionary definitions to help them solve translation problems. Bilingual dictionaries do have their place in the interpreter's library, of course, but they should be supplemented with more specialized dictionaries and reference works, as well as non-traditional sources of information. Gile (1995:133) identifies three different types of resources that interpreters and translators can consult: paper, human, and electronic. Listed below are resources that you will find helpful in your work as a court interpreter.

The Interpreter's Basic Library

There are certain reference works that should be present in every court interpreter's personal library for ongoing research:

1. A general monolingual dictionary in each of the interpreter's working languages
2. General bilingual dictionaries in each of the interpreter's language combinations
3. Monolingual legal dictionaries in each of the interpreter's working languages
4. Bilingual legal dictionaries in each of the interpreter's language combinations
5. Specialized bilingual or multilingual glossaries on topics of relevance to court cases
6. Legal texts such as civil and penal codes in each of the interpreter's working languages
7. Language references such as a thesaurus, style manual, grammar book, and dictionaries of synonyms and antonyms, phrases and collocations, slang, proverbs, and regionalisms in each of the interpreter's working languages
8. Periodicals of general interest such as newspapers and magazines in each of the interpreter's working languages

When considering the purchase of a dictionary or other reference work, which is no small investment, the following features should be evaluated: date of publication, country of origin, identity and credentials of author(s), reputation of publishing house, quality of binding and paper, and the presence or absence of usage notes regarding grammar, collocations, register, field of knowledge, and regionalisms. In the case of specialized dictionaries, it is also a good idea to look for "fillers", that is, general terms that could be found in any dictionary and are added simply to bulk up the volume. To test the reliability of a dictionary, look up a term you already know that is problematic and see how it is dealt with in this work.

Many novice interpreters wonder whether it is appropriate to bring dictionaries and glossaries to their interpreting assignments, fearing that their clients may doubt their competence. As pointed out in Chapter 4, just as legal professionals consult books in the courtroom (appellate reports, bench books, and codes, for example), interpreters need to bring the tools of their trade with them to the job. If you know in advance that a specific topic such as fingerprints or drug slang will be covered, you can come to the assignment prepared with specialized glossaries or notes from your research. It is always a good idea to have a comprehensive bilingual dictionary with you, in case an unknown term comes up unexpectedly or you suddenly have a memory lapse, something that afflicts all interpreters at one time or another. Portable electronic dictionaries are now available in many language combinations, making it easier to have thousands of terms at your fingertips.

Additional references that can be purchased or consulted in a public or university library:

1. Monolingual dictionaries on topics such as medicine, chemistry, business, accounting, finance, automotive terms, tools, pharmaceutical products, illegal drugs, and weapons
2. Bilingual dictionaries or glossaries on the topics listed above
3. Monolingual dictionaries and textbooks on specialized areas of the law such as contracts, property law, family law, probate, and labour relations
4. Visual dictionaries such as the Oxford-Duden series or the *What's What* series, which are published in many different languages
5. Textbooks for students of law, medicine, chemistry, law enforcement, accounting, or business
6. Publications issued by government agencies to inform the public about their programmes or about laws and regulations governing motor vehicles, labour relations, employment, job safety, pensions, housing, family matters, education, social welfare, health care, disability, and environmental law (in some countries these materials may be available in several languages)
7. Specialized periodicals such as journals and magazines targeted at professionals in the fields of law, medicine, and law enforcement

Other paper resources that can be useful for researching terminology, especially newly coined terms that have not yet made it into established publications, are newspaper and magazine advertisements, billboards, catalogues, and phone directories. To keep up with the latest usage, you should also try to listen to radio programming and watch television shows and movies in all of your working languages, if possible. The more times you come across a term in different resources, the more reliable the term is. Conversely, if you find a term in just one source and cannot verify it by cross-checking, you should be cautious about using it.

Human Resources

The above lists of references include works that ideally should be available to every interpreter, but in fact there is a paucity of reference material in some languages of limited diffusion. Indeed, some languages are not written at all, and it is virtually impossible to find reference materials in them. An alternative resource that should not be overlooked, even in the case of major languages, is human experts: Bilingual or monolingual professionals, elders, missionaries, and scholars, regardless of what country they live in, may be of assistance in your terminology research (though it may be time-consuming and expensive to contact them). Even the defendant or witness for whom you are interpreting, or his friends or relatives, may be consulted about the meaning or appropriate translation of a term, provided it is done with the knowledge of all the parties in the case. As with the case of printed resources, information obtained from human resources should be cross-checked for verification.

Electronic Resources

The advent of the Internet is a boon to translators and interpreters, who no longer have to travel to other countries or wait for publications to arrive in the mail in their quest for authentic resources. It would be pointless to try to list websites of interest to court interpreters, since there are so many, and since they are changing on a daily basis, but some general categories can be identified:

1. Terminology databases, of which Eurodicautom is the most well-known. Many international organizations maintain databases for their translation and interpretation staffs, and the public can gain access to them.
2. International organizations such as the United Nations, the International Court of Justice, the International Labour Organization, and the World Health Organization, from whose websites Internet users can download speeches and reports.
3. Private international organizations such as Amnesty International, Greenpeace, and Human Rights Watch, which also post reports on their homepages.
4. National institutions such as courts, legislatures, justice ministries and law enforcement agencies, which publish laws and regulations, information to educate the public, and glossaries.
5. Commercial entities that deal with legal matters, such as Court TV and private lawfirms, which post legal documents and information about prominent lawsuits and trials, as well as glossaries.
6. Bookstores and publishers, from which books and other materials can be purchased online.

7. Universities and their libraries. Some professors' and students' homepages have valuable links to other Internet sites in their area of expertise.
8. Public libraries, both national and local, such as the Library of Congress and the New York Public Library.
9. Professional associations of interpreters, translators, linguists, and others.
10. Listserves, chat rooms, and electronic bulletin boards help colleagues and speakers of a given language stay in contact through email. Translators and interpreters often post queries of the "how do you say ...?" or "what does ... mean?" sort on these lists and receive quick and reliable answers.

Continuing Education

It should be apparent by now that the work of a court interpreter includes a great deal of research. Early in your career you will spend much time and money developing your knowledge base and your library, but even though these expenditures will taper off as you gain experience, you will never abandon them entirely. Changes in language usage and the law, and the publication of new reference materials will oblige you to update your resources constantly. You may want to take courses in law, science, or medicine to gain more in-depth knowledge, or you may take advantage of seminars and workshops organized by professional associations. Reading crime novels and watching television programmes and movies about court cases is useful for keeping up with slang. Another way to engage in continuing education is by making field trips to workplaces or public institutions (such as a factory, a jail, or a crime lab), or participating in ride-along programmes offered by local police departments, to find out first-hand about the situations mentioned in the cases you interpret. Fortunately, most interpreters find that this professional development is an enjoyable aspect of their work, something that comes naturally to them as language lovers. In any case, it is an essential part of the job.

Suggested Activities

1. Invite guest speakers such as lawyers, criminalists, police officers, and judges to speak about specialized topics to your class.
2. Imagine that you have been assigned to interpret a trial involving money laundering and bank fraud. Explain how you will prepare for the case.
3. Clip photographs of vehicles, people, and buildings from magazines and newspapers, and use them as prompts for role-playing. For example, based on a picture of a car, one student will play a witness to an accident, another student will play the questioning attorney, and a third student will interpret. Pictures of people can be used for descriptions of suspects, and

pictures of buildings can be used to describe burglaries or robberies.

4. Make a list of the specific reference works you think every interpreter in your language combination should have.

5. Find out what professional translator and interpreter associations in your country or region offer continuing education activities.

6. Obtain a catalogue from a local institution of higher learning and identify classes that would be appropriate for a court interpreter to take.

Appendix A

Instructions to Parties in Interpreted Proceedings

The following instructions were developed by the New Jersey Supreme Court Task Force on Interpreter and Translation Services (1985:11-14). They are to be read by the judge or presiding judicial officer to the party or parties in question.

Notice to Defendants

1. We are going to have official court interpreters help us through these proceedings, and you should know what they can do and what they cannot do. Basically, court interpreters are here only to help us in the proceedings. They are not a party in this case, have no interest in this case, and will be completely neutral. Accordingly, they are working for neither [party A] nor [party B]. The official court interpreter's sole responsibility is to bridge our communication barrier.
2. The official court interpreters are not lawyers and are prohibited from giving legal advice. They are not social workers and are prohibited from providing social assistance to you or anyone else. Their only job is to interpret, translate written documents and do sight translation. So please do not ask court interpreters for legal advice or social assistance.
3. If you do not understand the court interpreter, please let me know. If the court interpreter leaves out much of what is going on, tell me that as well.
4. Do you have any questions about the role or responsibilities of the court interpreter?

Notice to Witness

1. I want you to understand the role of the court interpreter. The court interpreter is here only to interpret the questions that an attorney or I ask you and to interpret your responses. The court interpreter will say only what we or you say and will not add to your testimony, omit anything you say, or merely summarize.
2. If you do not understand the court interpreter, please say so immediately.
3. If you do not understand the question that was asked, ask the person who posed the question for a clarification of the question.
4. Remember that you are giving testimony to this court, not to the court

interpreter. Therefore please speak directly to the attorney or me. Do not address your replies to the court interpreter. Do not seek advice from or talk to the court interpreter.

5. Please speak in a loud, clear voice so that the entire court and not just the court interpreter can hear.

6. Finally, please do not formulate your answer to a question from counsel or me before you have heard the complete interpretation of the question in your language. Please await the full interpretation of the English before you reply.

7. Do you have any questions about the role or responsibilities of the court interpreter?

Notice to the Jurors

1. The court interpreter is an expert witness. Therefore you should treat the court interpretation rendered of the witness testimony as if the witness had spoken English and no court interpreter were present.

2. Do not give any weight to the fact that testimony is given in a language other than English. Do not allow the witness' inability to speak English to affect your view of the witness' credibility.

3. If any of you understand the language of the witness, disregard completely what the witness says in the other language. Consider as evidence *only* what is provided by the court interpreter in English.

4. [When the defendant requires a court interpreter] Do not attribute any prejudice to the fact that the defendant requires a court interpreter. This court seeks a fair trial of everyone regardless of the language they may speak. We will not permit bias against persons because they do not speak English.

Appendix B

Best Practice in Court Interpreting and Code of Conduct for Court Interpreters

The Committee for Legal Translators and Court Interpreters of the International Federation of Translators (FIT) adopted the "Best Practice in Court Interpreting" and the "Code of Conduct for Court Interpreters" at its meeting in Mons, Belgium, during the XVth World Congress of FIT in August 1999. A first draft of the texts had been presented at the Fourth International Forum and First European Congress on Court Interpreting and Legal Translation "Language is a Human Right", held in Graz, Austria, from 6 to 8 November 1998, and was discussed on a broader scale in the course of the year.

The "Best Practice in Court Interpreting" and the "Code of Conduct for Court Interpreters" are the contribution of the FIT Committee for Legal Translators and Court Interpreters to the "Code of Best Practice" of the European Translation Platform, EU Commission, Directorate XIII.

The two documents should serve as the "smallest common denominator" that can be applied throughout the world. Court interpreters and legal translators in different countries should feel free to translate the texts into their respective languages, add clauses in line with their national practice and distribute the documents among colleagues and other interested parties (for example, judges, lawyers, police and other authorities).

Best Practice in Court Interpreting

Introduction

The purpose of these recommendations is to guarantee the most favourable conditions for communication in court and to ensure that the co-operation between the interpreter[1] and the other parties functions as smoothly as possible.

A)   Interpreting assignment

1   Accepting an assignment
    1.1 When the interpreter is offered an assignment, the interpreter shall confirm his/her availability and take note of the particulars of the case in

---

[1] Whenever used here, the term interpreter refers to court interpreters, including sign-language interpreters, and legal translators.

question (date, place, subject, contact person) and shall arrange for the pertinent documents and other background material to be made available and shall also agree on the fees and the payment modalities, whenever necessary.

1.2 If the interpreter is unable to accept an assignment, he/she may recommend a colleague. The interpreter shall not accept an assignment and then request another interpreter to work in his/her stead without consulting with the client.

1.3 A written confirmation should be made of the assignment, preferably specifying the remuneration to be made to the interpreter in the event of the assignment being cancelled.

2   *Preparing for an assignment*

2.1 All the documents and other background material pertaining to the assignment shall be made available to the interpreter before the court session.

2.2 The interpreter shall study the material relating to the assignment and acquaint himself/herself with the necessary terminology.

3   *Performing an assignment*

3.1 Before the court session commences, the interpreter and the chairman of the court shall agree on how the interpretation is to be conducted, where the interpreter is to be placed and which type of interpreting mode is to be used (consecutive / simultaneous / chuchotage).

3.2 The interpreter is an impartial participant in the court session whose function is to render the proceedings accurately and reliably. The interpreter shall refrain from making personal comments during the proceedings, nor shall he/she be called upon to make such.

3.3 Interpreters shall dress appropriately for the environment in which they are required. They shall be punctual and shall behave correctly and impartially towards the persons involved (judge, lawyers, police, witnesses, accused, etc.).

3.4 The interpreter's fees shall be settled in a correct and timely fashion in accordance with the contract.

4   *Technical requirements*

4.1 Check the reactions of the client as you interpret to ensure that he/she has fully understood what you have said. If necessary, interrupt the speaker to avoid extremely long passages.

4.2 The direct mode ("I left the shop" and not "She says that she left the shop") shall be used when interpreting.

4.3 If you have to interrupt when two people are speaking at the same time, always go through the judge or the chairman of the court.

B)   Translation assignment

1   Accepting an assignment
1.1 The client and the translator shall agree on the timetable of the translation assignment and on the fees, etc. in advance and shall confirm the assignment in writing, whenever necessary. The translator shall not accept an assignment and then request another translator to take it on without consulting with the client.

2   Performing an assignment
2.1 The translator shall apply due diligence when doing the translation, consulting whatever sources necessary (dictionaries, encyclopaedias, experts, etc.)
2.2 The translator shall produce the translation in keeping with legal requirements (length of lines, lines/page, proper certification) and shall settle her/his fees similarly.
2.3 The translator shall consult with the client should there be obvious ambiguities and/or mistakes in the original text and never make any corrections himself/herself without previous consultation.
2.4 The translation shall be of high standard and neat in appearance.

Code of conduct for court interpreters

Introduction

The interpreter has a particular function in the court session. He/She shall render the proceedings both accurately and reliably.

Having regard to the fact that the court interpreter plays a key role in the search for the truth and that his/her work may affect the life and rights of others, the court interpreter accepts the following rights and obligations:

Article 1: Rights and obligations
1.1 In the practice of his/her profession, the court interpreter shall contribute actively to upholding fundamental rights and, in particular, the right to equality before the law.
1.2 The interpreter shall conscientiously perform his/her duties to the best of his/her ability and knowledge and shall accordingly make any reasonable effort to prepare an assignment.

1.3 The interpreter shall consult with the parties and/or the chairman of the court to ensure that the working conditions are appropriate.

Article 2: Confidentiality
The court interpreter shall not disclose any confidential matters to either party or to any third party.

Article 3: Misuse of information
The court interpreter shall not make personal use of any information obtained in the course of his/her duties nor assist any third party to do so.

Article 4: Impartiality and neutrality
The court interpreter shall at all times be neutral and impartial and shall not allow his/her personal attitudes or opinions to impinge upon the performance of his/her duties.

Article 5: Competence
The court interpreter shall only accept assignments for which he/she has the requisite knowledge and ability and which he/she can perform to a high standard. The interpreter shall be responsible for the correctness of his/her interpretation and shall correct any mistakes he/she makes.

Article 6: Co-operation with colleagues
The court interpreter shall at all times endeavour to co-operate with colleagues.

Bibliography

Adei, Christopher Y.D. (1981) *African Law South of the Sahara*, Clayton, MO: International Institute for Advanced Studies.

Akeeshoo, Atsainak (1993) 'Legal Interpreting in Canada's Eastern Arctic', *Meta* 38(1):35-37.

Arizona v. Natividad 111 Ariz. 191, 526 P.2d 730 (1974).

Bell, Roger T. (1991) *Translation and Translating: Theory and Practice*, London & New York: Longman.

Bell, Sherrill (1997) 'The Challenges of Setting and Monitoring the Standards of Community Interpreting: An Australian Perspective', in Silvana Carr, Roda Roberts, Aideen Dufour and Dini Steyn (eds) *The Critical Link: Interpreters in the Community*, Amsterdam & Philadelphia: John Benjamins, 93-108.

Berk-Seligson, Susan (1990) *The Bilingual Courtroom: Court Interpreters in the Judicial Process*, Chicago: University of Chicago Press.

------ (1999) 'The Impact of Court Interpreting on the Coerciveness of Leading Questions', *Forensic Linguistics, The International Journal of Speech, Language and the Law* 6(1):30-56.

Burris, Susan (1999) 'University Degree Program Steams Ahead', *The Polyglot* 29(1):3, 10.

Canadian Translators and Interpreters Council (CTIC) http://www.synapse.net/~ctic/e_certif.htm (7 May 99)

Carr, Silvana, Roda Roberts, Aideen Dufour and Dini Steyn (eds) (1997) *The Critical Link: Interpreters in the Community*, Amsterdam & Philadelphia: John Benjamins.

Catford, J. C. (1965) *A Linguistic Theory of Translation*, London: Oxford University Press.

Colegio de Traductores Públicos (1997) *Colegio de Traductores Públicos de la Ciudad de Buenos Aires*, Buenos Aires: Colegio de Traductores Públicos.

Colín Sánchez, Guillermo (1992) *Derecho mexicano de procedimientos penales*, Mexico City: Editorial Porrúa, S.A.

Colin, Joan and Ruth Morris (1996) *Interpreters and the Legal Process*, Winchester: Waterside Press.

Cooke, Michael (1995) 'Understood by All Concerned? Anglo/Aboriginal Legal Translation', in M. Morris (ed) *Translation and the Law*, American Translators Association Scholarly Monograph Series, Vol. VIII, Amsterdam & Philadelphia: John Benjamins, 37-63.

Corsellis, Ann (1995) *Non-English Speakers and the English Legal System*, Cambridge: The Institute of Criminology, University of Cambridge, Cropwood Occasional Papers No. 20.

------ (1997) 'Access to Public Service Interpreting: Why Is It necessary? Who Is Doing What?', *The Linguist* 36(5):144-146.

De Jongh, Elena (1992) *An Introduction to Court Interpreting: Theory and Practice*, Lanham, MD: University Press of America.

De Mas, Sarah (1999) 'Interpreting in the Criminal Justice Systems of Europe', in Liese Katschinka and Christine Springer (eds) *Proceedings of the Fourth International Forum and First European Congress on Court Interpreting and Legal Translation "Language Is a Human Right"*, Vienna: Fédération Internationale des Traducteurs, 12-14.

Derrett, J. Duncan M. (1963) *Introduction to Modern Hindu Law*, London: Oxford University Press.

Driesen, Christiane (1988) 'The Interpreters' Job – A Blow-by-blow Account', in Catriona Picken (ed) *ITI Conference 2 – Interpreters Mean Business*, London: Aslib London, 105-117.

------ (1989) 'Reformer l'interprétation judiciaire', *Parallèles, Cahiers de l'École de Traduction et d'Interprétation de l'Université de Genève* 11:93-98.

Edwards, Alicia (1995) *The Practice of Court Interpreting*, Amsterdam & Philadelphia: John Benjamins.

Erlich, Eugene and Marshall De Bruhl (compilers) (1996) *The International Thesaurus of Quotations*, London: Harper Collins Publishers.

Gaiba, Francesca (1998) *The Origins of Simultaneous Interpretation: The Nuremberg Trial*, Ottawa: University of Ottawa Press.

Gentile, Adolfo, Uldis Ozolins and Mary Vasilakakos (1996) *Liaison Interpreting, A Handbook*, Melbourne: Melbourne University Press.

Gile, Daniel (1995) *Basic Concepts and Models for Interpreter and Translator Training*, Amsterdam & Philadelphia: John Benjamins.

Glendon, Mary Ann, Michael Wallace Gordon and Paolo G. Carozza (1999) *Comparative Legal Traditions in a Nutshell*, St. Paul, MN: West Group.

González, Roseann, Victoria Vásquez and Holly Mikkelson (1991) *Fundamentals of Court Interpretation: Theory, Policy and Practice*, Durham, North Carolina: Carolina Academic Press.

Grusky, Lenne (1988) 'Using a New Technique for Witness Stand Interpreting', *ATA Chronicle* 18(10):12-13.

Gurevitch, Leonid (1997) 'Les traducteurs et la legislation', in Z. Rybinska (ed) *On the Practice of Legal and Specialised Translation*, Warsaw: The Polish Society of Economic, Legal and Court Translators TEPIS, 61-68.

Hale, Sandra (1997a) 'The Interpreter on Trial: Pragmatics in Court Interpreting', in Silvana Carr, Roda Roberts, Aideen Dufour and Dini Steyn (eds) *The Critical Link: Interpreters in the Community*, Amsterdam & Philadelphia: John Benjamins, 201-211.

------ (1997b) 'The Treatment of Register Variation in Court Interpreting', *The Translator* 3(1):39-54.

------ (1999) 'Interpreters' Treatment of Discourse Markers in Courtroom Questions', *Forensic Linguistics, The International Journal of Speech, Language and the Law* 6(1):57-82.

------ and Cesar Luzardo (1997) 'What Am I Expected to Do? The Interpreter's Ethical Dilemma, A Study of Arabic, Spanish and Vietnamese Speakers' Perceptions and Expectations of Interpreters', *Antipodean, The Australian Translation Journal* 1:10-16.

Hassan, Farooq (1981) *The Concept of State and Law in Islam*, Washington, D.C.: University Press of America, Inc.

Hatchard, John, Barbara Huber and Richard Vogler (eds) (1996) *Comparative Criminal Procedure*, London: British Institute of International and Comparative Law.

Heh, Yung-Chung and Hu Qian (1997) 'Over-the-Phone Interpretation: A New Way of Communication Between Speech Communities', in M. Jérôme-O'Keeffe (ed) *Proceedings of the 38th Annual Conference of the American Translators Association*, Alexandria, VA: American Translators Association, 51-62.

Hewitt, William (1995) *Court Interpretation: Model Guides for Policy and Practice in the State Courts*, Williamsburg, VA: National Center for State Courts.

Huber, Barbara (1996) 'Criminal Procedure in Germany', in John Hatchard, Barbara Huber and Richard Vogler (eds) *Comparative Criminal Procedure*, London: British Institute of International and Comparative Law, 96-175.

Hymes, Dell (1972) 'On Communicative Competence', in J. Pride and B. Holmes (eds) *Sociolinguistics: Selected Readings*, Harmondsworth: Penguin, 269-293.

Ilg, Gérard and Sylvie Lambert (1996) 'Teaching Consecutive Interpreting', *Interpreting* 1(1):69-99.

Inggs, Judith (1998) 'Current Developments in Court Interpreter Training in South Africa', *Proteus* 7(4):1, 3-4.

International Criminal Tribunal for Rwanda (ICTR) http://www.ictr.org/ (4 January 2000).

Ishay, Micheline (ed) (1997) *The Human Rights Reader: Major Political Essays, Speeches, and Documents From the Bible to the Present*, New York, London: Routledge.

Jacobs, Francis and Robin White (1996) *The European Convention on Human Rights*, Oxford: Clarendon Press.

Jacobsen, Bente (1999) 'Court Interpreting in Denmark: A Critical Perspective', in Liese Katschinka and Christine Springer (eds) *Proceedings of the Fourth International Forum and First European Congress on Court Interpreting and Legal Translation "Language Is a Human Right"*, Vienna: Fédération Internationale des Traducteurs, 56-63.

Jones, Roderick (1998) *Conference Interpreting Explained*, Manchester: St. Jerome.

Judicial Council of California (1998) *Court Interpreters Program* (pamphlet), San Francisco: Judicial Council of California, Administrative Office of the Courts.

Katschinka, Liese and Christine Springer (eds) (1999) *Proceedings of the Fourth International Forum and First European Congress on Court Interpreting and Legal Translation "Language Is a Human Right"*, Vienna: Fédération Internationale des Traducteurs.

Khoon, Wong Fook (1990) 'Court Interpreting in a Multiracial Society – the Malaysian Experience', in D. Bowen and M. Bowen (eds) *Interpreting – Yesterday, Today, and Tomorrow*, American Translators Association Scholarly Monograph Series, Volume IV, Binghamton, NY: State University of New York at Binghamton, 108-116.

Kingscott, Geoffrey (1997) 'Working to Solve South Africa's Language Problems',

Language Today, October.

Ladany, Laszlo (1992) *Law and Legality in China: The Testament of a China-watcher*, Honolulu: University of Hawaii Press.

Landaverde, Mariana (1999) 'Vernacular Languages of Guatemala', *ATA Chronicle* 28(10):56-57.

Leng, Shao-chuan and Hungdah Chiu (1985) *Criminal Justice in Post-Mao China: Analysis and Documents*, Albany, NY: State University of New York Press.

Levy, Jacob T. (1999) 'The Ethicist Who Isn't', *Reason*, December, 72-74.

Lewis v. United States 142 U.S. 370 (1892).

Loewy, Arnold H. (1987) *Criminal Law in a Nutshell*, St. Paul, MN: West Publishing Co.

Manganaras, Ioannis (1997) 'Court Interpreting in Greek Criminal Proceedings', in Z. Rybinska (ed) *On the Practice of Legal and Specialised Translation*, Warsaw: The Polish Society of Economic, Legal and Court Translators TEPIS, 85-102.

Márquez Villegas, Luis (1997) 'Orientaciones metodológicas para la realización de traducciones juradas', in Pedro San Gines Aguilar and Emilio Ortega Arjonilla (eds) *Introducción a la traducción jurídica y jurada (inglés-español)*, Granada: Editorial Comares, 99-114.

Martonova, Katerina (1997) 'Court Interpreting and Legal Translation in the Czech Republic', in Z. Rybinska (ed) *On the Practice of Legal and Specialised Translation*, Warsaw: The Polish Society of Economic, Legal and Court Translators TEPIS, 103-110.

Mehdi, Rubya (1994) *The Islamization of the Law in Pakistan*, Richmond, Surrey: Curzon Press Ltd.

Mellinkoff, David (1963) *The Language of the Law*, Boston & Toronto: Little, Brown & Co.

Merryman, John Henry and David S. Clark (1978) *Comparative Law: Western European and Latin American Legal Systems, Cases and Materials*, Indianapolis, New York, & Charlottesville, VA: The Bobbs-Merrill Co.

Mikkelson, Holly (1998) 'Towards a Redefinition of the Role of the Court Interpreter', *Interpreting* 3(1):21-45.

------ Victoria Vásquez and Roseann González (1989) 'Survey of Federally Certified Interpreters' Uses of Interpreting Techniques', Tucson: University of Arizona, Summer Institute for Court Interpretation.

Moeketsi, Rosemary (1999a) *Discourse in a Multilingual and Multicultural Courtroom: A Court Interpreter's Guide*, Pretoria: JL van Schaik.

------ (1999b) 'Redefining the Role of the South African Court Interpreter', *Proteus* 8 (3-4):12-15.

Morris, Ruth (1995a) 'The Moral Dilemmas of Court Interpreting', *The Translator* 1(1):25-46.

------ (1995b) 'Pragmatism, Precept and Passions: The Attitudes of English-Language Legal Systems to Non-English Speakers', in M. Morris (ed) *Translation and the Law*, American Translators Association Scholarly Monograph Series,

Volume VIII, Amsterdam & Philadelphia: John Benjamins, 263-279.

National Center for Interpretation Training, Research, and Policy (NCITRP) http://w3.arizona.edu/~ncitrp/ (7 May 99).

Neumann Solow, Sharon (1981) *Sign Language Interpreting: A Basic Resource Book*, Silver Spring, MD: The National Association of the Deaf.

New Jersey Supreme Court Task Force on Interpreter and Translation Services (1985) *Appendix to the Final Report*, Trenton, NJ: Administrative Office of the Courts.

Nicholson, Nancy and Bodil Martinsen (1997) 'Court Interpretation in Denmark', in Silvana Carr, Roda Roberts, Aideen Dufour and Dini Steyn (eds) *The Critical Link: Interpreters in the Community*, Amsterdam & Philadelphia: John Benjamins, 259-270.

Nida, Eugene and Charles Taber (1974) *The Theory and Practice of Translation*, New York: American Bible Society.

Niska, Helge (1995) 'Just Interpreting: Role Conflicts and Discourse Types in Court Interpreting', in M. Morris (ed) *Translation and the Law*, American Translators Association Scholarly Monograph Series, Volume VIII, Amsterdam & Philadelphia: John Benjamins, 293-316.

------ (1998) 'Testing Community Interpreters: A Theory, a Model and a Plea for Research', at http://lisa.tolk.su.se/00TEST.HTM (4 March 98).

Northwest Territories Justice (1993) *Des Territoires Du Nord-Ouest: Manuel Des Interprètes Judiciaires*, Northwest Territories Justice.

Ozolins, Uldis (1998) *Interpreting & Translating in Australia: Current Issues and International Comparisons*, Victoria: The National Languages and Literacy Institute of Australia.

People v. Chavez 124 Cal. App. 3d 215, 177 Cal. Rptr. 306 (Cal. App. Dist. 1, 1981).

Pöchhacker, Franz (1997) '"Is There Anybody Out There?" Community Interpreting in Austria', in Silvana Carr, Roda Roberts, Aideen Dufour and Dini Steyn (eds) *The Critical Link: Interpreters in the Community*, Amsterdam & Philadelphia: John Benjamins, 215-225.

Randmer, Virginia (1998) 'The Function of Public Translators in Brazil', translated by Donna Sandin, *ATA Chronicle* 28(8):39-40.

Registry of Interpreters for the Deaf (RID) (1995) *Specialist Certificate: Legal (SC:L) Examination Information Bulletin*, Silver Spring, MD: Registry of Interpreters for the Deaf.

Repa, Jindra (1991) 'Training and Certification of Court Interpreters in a Multicultural Society', *Meta* 36(4):595-605.

Rigney, Azucena (1999) 'Questioning in Interpreted Testimony', *Forensic Linguistics, The International Journal of Speech, Language and the Law* 6(1):83-108.

Rivezzi, Giovanna (1999) 'The Role of the Interpreter in the Criminal Case', in Liese Katschinka and Christine Springer (eds) *Proceedings of the Fourth International Forum and First European Congress on Court Interpreting and Legal Translation "Language Is a Human Right"*, Vienna: Fédération Internationale des Traducteurs (15-17).

Roberts, Roda (ed) (1981) *L'interprétation auprès des tribunaux*, Ottawa: Editions de l'Université d'Ottawa.

------ (1997) 'Community Interpreting Today and Tomorrow', in Silvana Carr, Roda Roberts, Aideen Dufour and Dini Steyn (eds) *The Critical Link: Interpreters in the Community*, Amsterdam & Philadelphia: John Benjamins, 7-26.

Rozan, Jean-François (1956) *La prise de notes en interprétation consécutive*, Geneva: Georg.

Rudolph, Lloyd I. and Susanne Haeber Rudolph (1967) *The Modernity of Tradition: Political Development in India*, Chicago & London: University of Chicago Press.

Rybinska, Zofia (ed) *On the Practice of Legal and Specialised Translation*, Warsaw: The Polish Society of Economic, Legal and Court Translators TEPIS.

Sammons, Susan (1993) 'Challenges in Minority Language Programming in Canada's Eastern Arctic: The Training of Aboriginal Language Interpreter-Translators', *Meta* 38(1):45-49.

Seleskovith, Danica (1968) *L'interprète dans les conférences internationales*, Paris: Minard Lettres Modernes.

Sherr, Daniel (1999) 'Interpreting in Spain and Colombia: Two Perspectives', *Proteus* 3(3-4):1, 3-4.

Supreme Court of Japan (1999) *A Guide to Court Procedures* http://www.courts.go.jp/english/procedure/index.htm (30 March 2000).

Szkodzinska, Anna (1997) 'The Sworn Translator in the Polish Legal System', in Z. Rybinska (ed) *On the Practice of Legal and Specialised Translation*, Warsaw: The Polish Society of Economic, Legal and Court Translators TEPIS, 120-129.

Tanaka, Hideo (ed) (1976) *The Japanese Legal System: Introductory Cases and Materials*, Tokyo: University of Tokyo Press.

Tsuda, Mamoru (1995) 'Interpreting and Translating for Filipino Suspects/Defendants in Japan: Selected Cases and Reflections of a Participant Observer', *Philippine Sociological Review* 43(1-4):139-160.

------ (1997) 'Human Rights Problems of Foreigners in Japan's Criminal Justice System', *Migrationworld* 25(1-2):22-25.

Tybulewicz, Albin (1997) 'ITI and its Law, Insurance, Finance and Court Networks', in Z. Rybinska (ed) *On the Practice of Legal and Specialised Translation*, Warsaw: The Polish Society of Economic, Legal and Court Translators TEPIS, 30-41.

University of Oslo (1996) *The Norwegian Interpreter Certification Project: Pilot Examination in Public Service Interpreting*, Oslo: The University of Oslo, Directorate of Immigration, Ministry of Local Government and Labour.

Vidal, Mirta (1997) 'New Study on Fatigue Confirms Need for Working in Teams', *Proteus* 4(1):1, 4-7.

------ (1998) 'Telephone Interpreting: Technological Advance or Due Process Impediment?', *Proteus* 7(3):1-6.

Vogler, Richard (1996) 'Criminal Procedure in France', in John Hatchard, Barbara Huber and Richard Vogler (eds) *Comparative Criminal Procedure*, London: British Institute of International and Comparative Law, 14-95.

Weber, Wilhelm (1984) *Training Translators and Conference Interpreters*, New York: Harcourt Brace Jovanovich, Inc.

Weller Ford, Georgeann (1992) 'Situación y perspectivas de lenguas indígenas, traducción e interpretación en México', in Michele Valiquette (ed) *Proceedings of Translating in North America - A Community of Interests*, Montreal: Regional Center for North America – RCNA/FIT, 126-139.

Wilss, Wolfram (1982) *The Science of Translation: Problems and Methods*, Tubingen, Germany: Guntar Narr Verlag.

Ziadeh, Farhat J. (1968) *Lawyers, the Rule of Law and Liberalism in Modern Egypt*, Stanford, CA: Hoover Institution on War, Revolution and Peace.